Maximizing Your Crown of Authority

Discovering Your Unique Personalization,
Authorization, and Organization
of Your Crown of Authority

By

Dr. Ron M. Horner

Maximizing Your Crown of Authority

Discovering Your Unique Personalization,
Authorization, and Organization
of Your Crown of Authority

By

Dr. Ron M. Horner

LifeSpring Publishing
PO Box 5847
Pinehurst, North Carolina 28374 USA
www.RonHorner.com

Maximizing Your Crown of Authority

Discovering Your Unique Personalization, Authorization, and Organization of Your Crown of Authority

Copyright © 2025 Dr. Ron M. Horner

Scripture is taken from the New King James Version®. Copyright © 1982 by Thomas Nelson. Used with permission. All rights reserved. (Unless otherwise noted.)

Scripture quotations marked (NLT) are taken from the Holy Bible, New Living Translation, copyright ©1996, 2004, 2015 by Tyndale House Foundation. Used by permission of Tyndale House Publishers, Carol Stream, Illinois 60188. All rights reserved.

Scripture marked (THE MIRROR) is taken from The Mirror Study Bible by Francois du Toit. Copyright © 2021 All Rights Reserved. Used by permission of The Author.

Scripture quotations marked (TPT) is taken from The Passion Translation®. Copyright ©2017, 2018 by Passion and Fire Ministries, Inc. Used by permission. All rights reserved. The PassionTranslation.com.

All rights reserved. This book is protected by the copyright laws of the United States of America. This book may not be copied or reprinted for commercial gain or profit. The use of short quotations or occasional page copying for personal, or group study is permitted and encouraged. Permission will be granted upon request.

Periodically, ChatGPT was used to compile research more quickly.

Trademarks are the property of their respective owners.

Requests for bulk sales discounts, editorial permissions, or other information should be addressed to:

LifeSpring Publishing
PO Box 5847
Pinehurst, NC 28374 USA

Additional copies available at: www.ronhorner.com

ISBN 13 TP: 978-1-953684-67-7
ISBN 13 eBook: 978-1-953684-68-4

Cover Design by Darian Horner Design
(www.darianhorner.com)
Image: 123rf.com #85093814

First Edition: July 2025

10 9 8 7 6 5 4 3 2 1 0

Printed in the United States of America

Table of Contents

Acknowledgments i

Characters Mentioned iii

Preface v

Chapter 1 Who Stole *Your* Crown? 1

Chapter 2 What Are the Crown Hunters? 9

Chapter 3 What is the Strategy of Isolation? 17

Chapter 4 Retrieving Lost Crowns 27

Chapter 5 Your Crown of Authority 41

Chapter 6 Have You Received Your Mantles? 57

Chapter 7 Are You Seated on Your Throne? 73

Chapter 8 Have You Exercised Your Dominion? 91

Chapter 9 Have You Embraced Your Anointing? ... 107

Chapter 10 Are You Wielding Your Scepter? 117

Chapter 11 Are You Demonstrating The Glory? ... 125

Chapter 12 Are You Accessing the Resources? 141

Chapter 13 The Crown of Life 149

Chapter 14 The Crown of the Lamb 159

Chapter 15 Obtaining the Crown of a Sound Mind . 173

Chapter 16 Maintaining Your Crown 181

Chapter 17 Epilogue 189

Appendix.. 191

    Learning to Live Spirit First 193

    Resources from LifeSpring 201

    Description 207

    About the Author... 209

    Other Books by Dr. Ron M. Horner 211

Acknowledgments

When I first studied the subject of crowns, I never imagined how much information was on the subject—directly or indirectly. Getting this information with Stephanie Stanfill has been invaluable. She serves as a very capable seer with a heart for the Father. I honor her for her service.

Adina, my wife, was also helpful in giving me space to write when the portal of writing opened for this book, so I would not be disturbed.

Many blessings to you both, and may you maximize *your crowns,* too!

———— ∞ ————

Characters Mentioned

Adina – Dr. Ron Horner's beautiful wife, co-founder, and Chief Financial Officer of LifeSpring

Einstein – the physicist of 20th-century fame.

Ezekiel – the Chief Angel over our ministry.

Lydia – our Chief Business Advisor for LifeSpring

Malcolm – a man in white who tutors us in the things of Heaven.

Mary Magdalene – the woman who washed Jesus' feet with her hair.

Stephanie – serves as the Chief Operating Officer of LifeSpring International Ministries, Inc.

Lady Wisdom – the entity that carries and imparts wisdom. See Proverbs 8.

Preface

New Seasons

Stephanie prayed,

Father, we thank you for this opportunity to step into the realms of Heaven through your son Jesus.

She asked, "What does Heaven have to say to us today? We're grateful for the crown's revelation.

"I see that we are standing at the base of a large boulder. I see Einstein, and he's taking measurements of this boulder. Hi, Einstein. What is this?"

Einstein replied, "This is a picture of **your rock and foundation**. I can't get the measurements. There's no way to measure."

Stephanie noted, "Well, the Word says something about no height or depth. What's the scripture?"

Romans 8:38-39:

> *For I am persuaded that neither death nor life, nor angels nor principalities nor powers, nor things present nor things to come,* ³⁹ ***nor height nor depth****, nor any other created thing, shall be able to separate us from the love of God which is in Christ Jesus our Lord. (Emphasis mine)*

"Would you say this size boulder could crush your enemies?" Einstein inquired.

Stephanie replied, "I do, and it would. Wow, Einstein!"

With one hand, he picked up this boulder.

Einstein stated, "His yoke is easy, and His burden is light."

Stephanie remarked, "I'm realizing that this boulder is a crown he's holding in his hand." When he put it back down on the ground, one of the prisms of the crown opened like a door, and Einstein instructed me to come inside it.

"It is all crystal. It is beautiful. What did you want to show us about this?"

Einstein noted, "Crowns from the Lord cause you to enter new seasons.

Crowns from the Lord cause you to enter new seasons.

"There have been many seasons that have been stolen from the sons.

This revelation will cause the sons to walk in new seasons. This is quantum.

"The seasons of the past that were stolen from the sons, the stolen seasons will come back in revelation to the sons—in reorientation. Door after door after door, opportunity after opportunity after opportunity. (Things said in 3's means to pay attention). Season by season. Glory and more glory in the vivid imaginations, a thrusting forward. Leaning over to make a point, he said, "This is much different from the thrusting of the dragon. This is acceleration, a leaping, a crossing over of time and space. You have entered a new season.

You have entered a new season.

"Take on these crowns. These are new doors. Many doors that were previously closed are now opening. The climate is changing. (Even though we had just entered spring, Heaven was not speaking of the climate or weather.)

Seasons of your life have changed, and are changing in these doors. This is a principle.

"Just as a theme park or county fair might have a house of mirrors, and you can look into them and see endlessly, so it is for the sons in this season. There is a new dimension. It's a new door, a new opportunity. That's what this crown revelation has given you.

From The Passion Translation, Romans 8:38-39:

*^{38} So now I live with the confidence that **there is nothing in the universe with the power to separate us from God's love**. I'm convinced that his love will triumph over death, life's troubles, fallen angels or dark rulers in our heavens, **there is nothing in our present or future circumstances that can weaken His love**. ^{39} There is no power above us or beneath us. **No power that could ever be found in the universe that can distance us from God's passionate love**, which is lavished upon us through our Lord Jesus, the Anointed One. (TPT) (Emphasis mine)*

From the Mirror Bible, Romans 8:38-39:

*^{38} This is my conviction. No threat, whether it be in death or life, be it celestial messengers, demon powers or political principalities. Nothing known to us at this time or even in the unknown future. ^{39} **No dimension of any calculation in time or space, nor any device yet to be invented has what it takes** to separate us from*

the love of God unveiled in our Lord Jesus Christ. (MIRROR) (Emphasis mine)

When it says, "nor any device," so many people are caught up in the evil technologies and devices and chains of bondage, and that scripture in that translation handles all of that fear in one scripture. He is above all darkness, period."

One final thing. I request access to the Court of Crowns on your behalf, and I ask that the Crown of Revelation Receiver be granted to you so that you have the capacity to receive the revelation in this book.

As an act of faith, receive that crown from the Father and all it entails. This will assist you in absorbing the material in this book.

———— ∞ ————

Chapter 1

Who Stole *Your* Crown?

The dysfunction you see in society results from wearing the wrong crowns and losing the right crowns. Crowns metaphorically symbolize authority and dominion. We refer to individuals at the top of their game as kings. Kings wear crowns. Kings have dominion, not just geographically but in other realms as well. However, others may be jealous of you and/or the crowns you wear. They may not know it is due to a crown, but their spirit knows.

Many years ago, my wife and I were summoned to a church board meeting to address accusations we were unaware of. Apparently, the pastor's mother and a few others made some accusations against us. The church board meeting was nothing short of a tribunal where we were tried, convicted, and sentenced without even knowing the charges. We were seen as guilty even before it began. The meeting was simply a poorly performed formality.

The goal of our enemy was to steal the crowns we possessed. In particular, the church tribunal was after our Crown of Zeal (although they did not label it as such). One of the charges was that we were "too zealous." However, I have noticed over the years that whenever someone is seen as overzealous, the accusations often come from someone with far less zeal than the accused. They are accusing you of something they aren't likely to be accused of, or they are motivated by jealousy because you possess something they covet. On other issues, they often accuse you of something they are guilty of themselves. They are simply trying to deflect their own guilt onto you.

As a result of that meeting, our Crown of Zeal was stolen from us (among other crowns), although we did not recognize it at the time. Thereafter, we became far more cautious of leaders and bored church boards and were much "tamer" than we may have been before. Those of you who know me recognize that I am not one to go shouting, jumping, and hollering anyway. I have never been, but a level of energy and strength was gone.

We didn't know how to define what had happened to us until we began studying the concept of crowns and their significance. Other crowns were stolen that day, but we have started the reclamation process now that we know what to call what happened.

> *Knowing what has been lost is crucial to know what to go after and retrieve.*

Other results of that board meeting were the placement on our heads of an ungodly Crown of Disgrace. I refused to wear that crown, although my wife struggled with its impact on her for several years. I have a personal philosophy: "If I didn't commit the crime, I'm not going to do the time." If I'm not guilty of something, I won't live in the bondage of the accusation as if I had committed the crime. That philosophy has been helpful throughout the years.

Now, we know the power of crowns and the ability of ungodly crowns to try to reproduce in you whatever they are, but by the same token, godly crowns can produce in you *whatever they are*. A Crown of Righteousness will help produce righteousness in you, a Crown of Peace will produce peace, and a Crown of Rejoicing will produce joy in you. On the other hand, the inferior Crown of Dishonor will produce situations where you are dishonored, while an inferior Crown of Disgrace will attempt to instill in you times when you are disgraced. Whatever the source, it will dictate the fruit of the crown.

You may have gone through a similar experience. You may have faced a church tribunal. You may have experienced spiritual abuse on that level or even worse. We want to help you recover what was taken from you.

Maybe, as a child, a sibling or parent may have been used to steal your crown. An event resulted in a loss of strength or confidence in a particular area.

In my book, *Embracing Your Crown of Authority*,[1] I show how Elijah lost crowns following the encounter with the prophets of Baal. He did not pace himself for recovery after the massacre of the false prophets. Extreme weariness is a setup to steal your crowns from you. When Elijah saw what Jezebel had planned for him, it was as if he had suddenly packed up and left town, leaving his crowns behind. He let fear of Jezebel's threats rob him of the crowns he wore. Fortunately, over the next few weeks, he regained them, but the mantle he wore was soon passed on to his successor.

Be aware of attacks to steal your crowns when you are physically or emotionally tired.

When we wear the right crowns, we have strength and anointing in that arena, and when that crown is

---

[1] *Embracing Your Crown of Authority* by Dr. Ron M Horner, LifeSpring Publishing (2025).

taken from us, we no longer have the strength or confidence that the crown provided.

When someone loses all their godly crowns (and you don't have to be a believer in Jesus to have godly crowns), they are prime candidates for depression—even suicide. The more ungodly crowns one wears, the worse off they are. Particularly if they are wearing some of the false crowns of the red dragon in Revelation 12.

As sons of God, we need to identify what crowns have been lost, forfeited, or stolen from us and reclaim them, along with their rightful authority to operate in our lives. We must also recognize that we may have helped the process by losing crowns, forfeiting them by laying them down, even casting them to the ground, and or rejecting them. At other times, we may have been complicit in their loss by our agreement with hell or a negative declaration on some level. To say that it is too hard to live from the strength of a particular crown is to misunderstand the complete package of what the Father has provided when godly crowns are bestowed upon us.

Many times, we are led to believe that a crown is too hard to attain because it will cost us more than we are willing to pay.

The Apostle Paul was fully convinced of what he wrote to the Roman believers in Romans 8:

Nothing can separate us from the love of God.

Anything he had to endure, any price he had to pay, was a small thing compared to the new level of the Glory of God he would then experience. He had calculated the cost to the point that it was no longer a consideration for him. We must also be firmly convinced that the new crowns we can obtain are far more valuable than the supposed or imagined cost. We don't understand that possessing some crowns is part of our scroll.

These crowns are ours to obtain, wear, and walk in the strength of.

In 1 Timothy 3, we read about the qualifications for a deacon. The position of a deacon comes with an accompanying crown designed to help you live out the lifestyle of a deacon, the Crown of a Deacon.

A few verses prior, Paul lists qualifications for bishops. He points out that the position of bishop could be desired. It wasn't a calling but an office one could desire and be released into. With the office of a bishop, an accompanying crown would come. In 1 Timothy 3:1, we read:

If a man desires *the position of a bishop, he desires a good work. (Emphasis mine)*

Contrary to popular belief, that office has nothing to do with calling. You can desire certain offices just as you can desire particular crowns and obtain them in that manner.

> *Some crowns come because of the price you paid to get them.*

Other crowns come regardless of the perceived cost, while others come so you will have the strength to endure the challenges you will face as part of your scroll.

Most of us have been taught that we can only get crowns when we reach Heaven, but I see limited (or at least unperceived) benefits in waiting until then. If a crown has with it a mantle, a dominion, a throne, as well as other things, I need them here, on this side of eternity. I'm going to desire them now, not merely later. I may want them in Heaven, too, but I need them now. How about you?

We will discuss retrieving lost, stolen, or forfeited crowns in more detail later in this book. Don't worry, you'll get your crowns back! It won't be long.

―――― ∞ ――――

Chapter 2

What Are the Crown Hunters?

Although the old saying, "if all you have is a hammer, everything is a nail," is apropos at times, the book of Jeremiah says, "Is not my word like a hammer?"

Jeremiah 23:29:

> 'Is not My word like a fire?' says the LORD, and like a hammer that breaks the rock in pieces?

I heard the Father speak this to me:

> *Yes, it is. Hammers impact things. Hammers reshape things. Hammers are helpful to fit things together. Hammers are versatile tools for a wide range of construction tasks. They help tear down old things. EVERYTHING is a nail when you have a hammer.*
>
> *My Word impacts things, reshapes things, and helps fit things together. Hammers are helpful*

when building and when tearing things down. Hammers help change things.

You have begun to see that I have either spoken of crowns or alluded to them repeatedly in Scripture. As the sons get the revelation inside them, their souls may want to change the subject. The soul must be instructed and made to comply with what the spirit of man is hungering for. It is now hungry to understand what happened to them years ago, months ago, or days ago when they suddenly had a sense of loss that they may not have been able to define.

Crown hunters took advantage of the fact that the victims did not know what they were carrying. So, when the crown was knocked off their heads, stolen from them, or even laid down in a period of despair, the very blueprint of their lives was affected. What I have said to them has been delayed in their lives because of the work of the crown hunters.

These crown hunters are the foxes spoken of in Lamentations[2] and the Song of Songs[3]. They were feeding their flesh at the expense of their spirits. Many of the faithful never transition into

---

[2] Lamentations 5:18

[3] Song of Solomon 2:15

sonship because their crowns have been stolen or removed from them due to traumas.

LifeSpring is about helping people receive freedom and doing it more effectively.

That has been the cry of the heart for the leadership of LifeSpring.

We are firmly convinced that it doesn't take years to get someone free of SRA, DID, or any of the other alphabet soups that people find themselves in. Invite Jesus into the situation, and He will do things remarkably fast.

The Role of Crowns

Father also spoke this to me:

Understanding the role of crowns is crucial for healing people quickly and effectively. It affects timelines. It affects emotions. It affects many people's way of life. Crowns connect to one's purpose, much like the light switch restricts or releases energy flow into your home to illuminate or darken a room.

When crowns are restored, and the reauthorization is brought to bear, the purpose of that crown becomes easier to see. Strength will come related to the crown. A hope will come, a release of joy will come, and a release of an anointing to bring change will come. I have designed it so that when the Crowns of Zeal and Crowns of Righteousness are entirely in place, my sons can begin to accomplish things they have struggled to achieve before.

Many have testified of the breakthroughs and the hope they are sensing as they regain their crowns. More will be able to testify in future days of what I am doing in their lives.

Many have been preoccupied with provision-related matters, but understanding the power of the Crown of Righteousness and its far-reaching impact and fully integrating its operation into one's life will bring about significant changes.

The enemy wants to steal from your life the primary attributes of the Kingdom of God.

Romans 14:17:

> *For the Kingdom of God is not eating and drinking but righteousness, peace, and joy in the Holy Spirit.*

You have learned about the Crown of Righteousness and its benefits. You wear that as a son and as a faithful one. However, the enemy still seeks to remove it from your life, as explained by the Crown of Antichrist. That crown is about removing the sense of foundness you experience in Jesus and bringing you back to the state of lostness you once had; however, at that point, you have tasted of the heavenly gift and the power of things to come, and by embracing that crown, you have returned to that state. (Hebrews 6:4-6)[4]

That is not My plan nor desire for My sons and faithful ones.[5]

The placing upon one's head
of the Crown of Everlasting
and the Crown of Purpose
will begin the restoration process
for many whose hope
has been deferred.

When Hope Is Lost

When hope is lost, joy is missing, righteousness is disregarded, and peace is absent. Place upon the heads of my sons and faithful ones the Crown of Peace, the Crown of Joy, and restore the

---

[4] Learn about these crowns in my book *Embracing Your Crown of Authority*, LifeSpring Publishing (2025).

[5] Faithful ones are those who are born again but have yet to embrace their sonship.

Crown of Righteousness if it has been knocked askew upon them. Release to them from the storehouses of Heaven the Crown of Everlasting. Call them back to the awakening of their purpose.

Many need the restoration of the Crown of the Tree of Life, for My Word says, 'Hope deferred makes a heart sick, but a desire fulfilled is a tree of life.'[6] The heart no longer needs to be sick when the Crown of the Tree of Life is restored or placed upon them for the first time. I want all my sons to walk in fullness. I want them all to walk in the fullness of the Kingdom of God...in righteousness, peace, and joy—great joy! Great, great joy!

Joy will be a defining factor for many, for they will see My sons walking in that place under the Crown of Rejoicing and say, 'Why are you so joyful?' They will say, 'Because I am crowned with Joy? Wouldn't you like to be?'

The workings of the false crowns through others have sought to silence the sons: Ask my sons, where have you been silenced? What have you lost joy in doing?

---

[6] Proverbs 13:12

You are sons placed on this planet to solve particular sets of problems. You must be crowned with zeal and with knowledge of your purpose to be able to solve those problems. You must be walking in the strength of the Crown of Righteousness. Understand that the Father doesn't hold you accountable for what Jesus paid for on your behalf. He is not looking to judge you but to justify you and what He has already accomplished in your life.

Crown hunters have been assigned to steal your crowns. Part of the process of these foxes is to mock you into silence and submission. Never give place to the mockers.

Remember, Psalm 1:1 says:

> *Blessed is the man who walks **NOT** in the counsel of the ungodly, nor stands in the way of sinners or sits in the seat of the mockers—(those that have embraced inferior crowns). (Emphasis mine)*

Each of these people in that passage has embraced the wrong crown.

Remember, there are Superior Crowns and inferior crowns. If you have accepted an inferior crown, quickly repent and remove it from your head. Ask the angels to clean up the debris from your realm and step out of the jurisdiction of the inferior crown that has been placed around your life. The physical act of stepping out of one place and into a new place will be necessary for many to realize the distinction between where they have been and where they need to be as they walk in the proper jurisdictions.

Those consumed with the pronouncements of darkness over their life have had their crowns stolen. Speak to them of removing crowns that deny the anointing in their lives—the false Crown of Antichrist. The false Crown of Antichrist pronounces to them in piercing frequencies that Jesus is not enough. What they have experienced is more than they can handle. They are beyond hope—their hope has been deferred. These pronouncements are the voices of the Crown of Antichrist. Remove it from their head so they can think clearly about where the Crown of a Sound Mind can start functioning.

I have not given you a false Crown of Fear but a Crown of Power, a Crown of Love, and a Crown of a Sound Mind. Let them rest upon your head and have the Crown of Fear destroyed from your life. Walk in the fullness provided to My sons.

———— ∞ ————

Chapter 3

What is the Strategy of Isolation?

The Mirror Bible gives an interesting but valuable interpretation of Revelation 3:11:

> *Do not let tough times make me seem distant from you. I am at hand - see my nearness, not my absence. And don't let temporal setbacks diminish your own authority either. Remember that you call the shots; you wear the crown. My crown endorses your crown (or "Let nothing take your crown"). (MIRROR)*

An often-used strategy of Satan to defeat you is to isolate you. If he can isolate you, he can captivate you. You have all seen nature documentaries where a lion is seeking its next meal and looks for prey that is isolated from the others, or one that is walking with a limp, or perhaps a young animal to make dinner. When the lion gives chase, it seeks to separate the prey from the herd. The enemy does that to people—he separates them from others through accusations, whispers, innuendos, and other means. If we don't govern the whispers, and by that, I mean when we don't discern their origin, we will allow them to grow in our minds.

We have angels over our realms available to us, so when thoughts come into your mind that need to be governed, enlist the help of your soul realm angels to capture every thought and bring it into captivity.

2 Corinthians 10:4-6:

> [4] *For **the weapons** of our warfare **are not carnal** but mighty in God for pulling down strongholds, [5] **casting down arguments and every high thing that exalts itself against the knowledge of God, bringing every thought into captivity to the obedience of Christ,** [6] and being ready to punish all disobedience when your obedience is fulfilled. (Emphasis mine)*

In 2 Corinthians 2:11, Paul wrote:

> *The strategy of every accusation is to **divide** and **dominate**. (MIRROR)*

Accusations seek to divide you from the truth about a person or situation. If they can divide you from the truth, they can begin to dominate the relationships involved. Once you are subjected to an accusation about someone, it is difficult to forget that accusation when dealing with that person. The accusation will always be in the back of your mind. That is why the teaching in my book *The Four Keys to Defeating Accusations*[7] is so crucial. When we learn to govern the whispers, we learn:

- Where are they coming from? (Heaven, hell, people?)
- What is their endgame? (to divide you and the other party(ies) from the truth about the situation and dominate the relationship improperly).

There may have been a hint of truth, but if 99% of the information is false, it essentially invalidates the 1% of truth, as that "truth" is probably taken out of context and doesn't provide a clear picture.

When you are isolated, you remove the strength of the group from yourself, and the strength you provide is removed from the group. There is a certain safety in numbers that needs to be appreciated. Often, within a group, there is collective wisdom that can be utilized. Observe the more senior individuals in a group and note how they react to whispers or don't react. Their responses can reveal how they have handled similar situations and how they understand the potential outcome. Some outcomes are predictable.

---

[7] *Four Keys to Defeating Accusations – Second Edition* by Dr. Ron M. Horner. LifeSpring Publishing (ronhorner.com) (2024).

They tell you in mystery writing that there are typically fewer than a dozen basic plots that all mysteries employ. They will use one of those 11 or 12 plots, which explains the predictability of many books and movies. It is no different when it comes to whispers. A limited number of likely scenarios are likely to play out.

When the lion attacks, it often targets the neck area of the animal, as this provides the largest flesh area without the intrusion of the skeletal structure that would hinder the depth of the bite. It also wants to hinder the prey's ability to maneuver. The lion will hang on to their prey for as long as possible, seeking to exhaust them from carrying the extra weight of the lion as they try to escape.

In your own life, when a whisper is not governed, it often becomes an accusation that must be recognized and dismantled. When not dismantled, it becomes an extra weight that will eventually wear you out.

Amos 3:11:

> *Therefore thus says the Lord GOD: 'An adversary shall be all around the land; he shall **sap your strength from you, and your palaces shall be plundered.**' (NLT) (Emphasis mine)*

We are told to:

1. Agree with your adversary[8]
2. Confess the accusation is sin
3. Repent of the sin
4. Ask for Jesus' blood to cover the accusation and all its ramifications.

Accusations embraced become sins to be repented of.

---

*When I embrace an accusation,
I am choosing to say something
about someone or something
the Father is not likely
saying about them.*

Sin ensnares and hinders our ability to run the race set before us.

Hebrews 12:1-2:

> *[1] Therefore we also, since we are surrounded by so great a cloud of witnesses, let us **lay aside every weight**, and the **sin which so easily ensnares** us, and **let us run with endurance the race that is set before us**, [2] looking unto*

---

[8] Matthew 5:25: Agree with your adversary quickly, while you are on the way with him, lest your adversary deliver you to the judge, the judge hand you over to the officer, and you be thrown into prison.

Jesus, the author and finisher of our faith, who for the joy that was set before Him endured the cross, despising the shame, and has sat down at the right hand of the throne of God.

Jesus is the one who began writing our book, and He is the one who signs it, "The End."

You are NOT Forgotten nor Forsaken

Regardless of what your enemy says about you or someone else, you are not forgotten by the Father.

Revelation 3:11:

> **Do not let tough times make me seem distant from you.** *I am at hand - see my nearness, not my absence. And don't let temporal setbacks diminish your own authority either.*

The enemy wants you to think the Father has forgotten you AND forsaken you.

We are promised in Romans 8:35, 37-39:

> [35] **Who shall separate us** *from the love of Christ? Shall tribulation, or distress, or persecution, or famine, or nakedness, or peril, or sword?*

*³⁷ Yet in all these things **we are more than conquerors through Him** who loved us.*

*³⁸ For I am persuaded that neither <u>death</u> nor <u>life</u>, nor <u>angels</u> nor <u>principalities</u> nor <u>powers</u>, nor <u>things present</u> nor <u>things to come</u>, ³⁹ nor <u>height</u> nor <u>depth</u>, nor <u>any other created thing</u>, **shall be able to separate us from the love of God** which is in Christ Jesus our Lord. (Emphasis mine)*

Read the same passage from the Mirror Bible:

*³⁵ **What will it take to distance us from the love of Christ?** You name any potential calamity: intense pressure of the worst possible kind, claustrophobia, persecution, destitution, loneliness, extreme exposure, life-threatening danger, or war?*

*³⁷ On the contrary, in the thick of these things our triumph remains beyond dispute. His love has placed us above the reach of any onslaught. ³⁸ This is my conviction; no threat whether it be in **death** or **life**; be it **celestial messengers, demon powers** or **political principalities, nothing known to us at this time, or even in the unknown future;** ³⁹ no **dimension of any calculation in time or space,** nor **any device yet to be invented,** has what it takes to separate us from the love of God unveiled in our Lord, Jesus Christ. (Emphasis mine)*

Hebrews 13:5-6:

⁵ For He Himself has said, 'I will never leave you nor forsake you.'

*⁶ So we may **boldly say**: 'The Lord is my helper; I will not fear. What can man do to me?' (Emphasis mine)*

Jesus said in Matthew 28:20:

Lo, I am with you always, even to the end of the age.

Kenneth E. Hagin once said:

We have to decide that God's Word is more true than our thinking.

We must settle that if He said, "He would not leave us," *then he won't!*

If He said, "I am with you always," *then He is!*

There is comfort in knowing you are never alone. Holy Spirit doesn't take a coffee break. No device invented can separate us from His love. No dimension of ANY calculation in time or space can separate us.

The verse *"I will never leave you nor forsake you"* comes from Deuteronomy 31:7-8:

⁷ Then Moses called Joshua and said to him in the sight of all Israel, 'Be strong and of good courage, for you must go with this people to the land which the LORD has sworn to their fathers to give them, and you shall cause them to inherit it.

*⁸ And the LORD, He is the One who **goes before you**. He will **be with you**, He will **not leave you** nor **forsake you**; do not fear nor be dismayed.'* *(Emphasis mine)*

Satan lost his crowns at the rebellion, so if the enemy can get you to agree with him that the Father has forsaken you, he will have stolen your Crown of Sonship and will parade it around, bragging about how he defeated you.

He wants your crown, and he wants what your crown represents—authority over him!

The enemy wants to separate you from your authority.

———— ∞ ————

Chapter 4

Retrieving Lost Crowns

To maximize what Heaven provides through a crown, we need to understand what those provisions are. The typical components of a crown include:

- **The Crown** – The obvious representation of the authority you carry in the particular arena your crown encompasses.
- **The Mantle** – Coupled with the Anointing, this is the empowerment of Heaven for what your Crown represents and provides.
- **The Throne** – The seated place of your dominion.
- **The Anointing** that accompanies the crown. It is proof of the authorization of the Crown by Heaven.
- **The Scepter** – a secondary symbol of your Throne.
- **The Dominion** that the crown represents.

- **The Glory** – the expression of Heaven that you carry as you wear your crown.
- **The Resources** – the natural and supernatural things you will need to accomplish the mantle of a crown.

I'll discuss these in greater depth later.

If Satan gets your crown he gets all of the above.

If you drive on the highway and have a flat tire, you don't abandon the vehicle. You change the tire and continue to your destination. It's the same in our Christian walk. If we make a mistake, it's a temporary setback, not a permanent condition. So you messed up. Repent, get up, and go on. The enemy will say that you have disqualified yourself from all the Father has for you, which may be true as long as the setback is not repented. However, once it is repented of, move on. Don't even pause. Move forward without hesitation!

Setbacks that are unrepented of **will** diminish your authority, but once repented of, the authority is restored in full force. Recognize that the enemy uses those occasions to try to steal your crown. If it got knocked askew, repent and place it firmly back on your head. Then, request the reauthorization of the authority of that crown. As the passage says, *"Don't let **anyone** steal your crown!"*

The Mirror Translation says in Revelation 3:

Remember that <u>you</u> call the shots; <u>you</u> wear the crown. (Emphasis mine)

You choose to deal with the setbacks and move forward. Heaven isn't stopping you, and hell CANNOT stop you! Only you can stop you.

Finally, it says,

My crown endorses your crown.

Because Jesus wears His crown, you are fully qualified to wear your crown. He paid the price; he paved the way.

He bought your victory IN FULL at the resurrection.

WEAR YOUR CROWN!

If you find these things difficult, it may be that Satan has already stolen some crowns from you:

- A Crown of Fortitude
- A Crown of Hope
- A Crown of Strength
- A Crown of Determination
- A Crown of Overcomer

Let's get them back!

Where we contributed to the loss or forfeiture, simply repent, then go to the Court of Crowns and receive renewed authorization for the authority that has been lost. Request that of the court, having done repentance for losing that crown. Then, commission the angels to begin bringing in what has been lost and fill the capacity. That capacity can also be enlarged.

Stephanie prayed:

Where we laid down our authority, or our generations did, and stepped out of our authority, we want to acknowledge that and take responsibility for it. We repent of it and ask that the authority and territory that had been taken be re-established in the name of Jesus.

Where others were involved in the loss or theft of our crowns, we forgive them, bless them, and release them. We ask for the restoration of the crowns.

We ask this court for renewed authorization of the authority that was lost due to the forfeiture or loss of our crown(s).

We also thank the court for the establishment and the capacity of the promised land that have not been able to come forth because of us not governing correctly as sons, but we now understand the capacity of what we are and whose we are as we indeed take in the territory, the lands, the inheritances, and all that has been established here in the name of Jesus.

We commission the angels to bring these things from this place into the natural realm on behalf of the sons so that we may be good stewards of what you give us.

As Stephanie prayed, she got a bird's eye view of the Court of Crowns and realized we were inside a crown.

Retrieval of Lost, Forfeited, or Stolen Crowns

You need to determine if Satan has stolen crowns from you. How? Simply ask. Has Satan stolen crowns from me?

The answer should be simple to decide on. "Yes, or no?" If yes, which I'm sure it will be, then begin to specify various crowns that you feel were taken from you. Once you have a sense of what you have lost due to his thievery,

Steps of Retrieval for Crowns in a Trophy Room

1. Access the Court of Crowns.
2. Repent for our part in the loss of the crown(s)
3. Request the restoration of those crowns you lost.
4. Commission angels to retrieve the crowns from the trophy room of hell and bring them to you.
5. Take them from the angels.
6. Put them on your head.

7. Request the re-authorization of those crowns upon your life.
8. Commission angels to retrieve what was lost or stolen from you, from the north, south, east, west, and every age, realm, and dimension.

Finally, we must understand that a continual association with the victory Jesus purchased for us is necessary to maintain your crown(s).

Revelation 3:12:

It is in your individual, **continual association with your[9] victory in me** *that I will make you to be like a strong pillar in the inner shrine of God's sanctuary, supporting the entire structure of my God-habitation within you. A place to be your permanent abode from whence you will never have to depart. And I will engrave upon you the name of my God, also the name of the city [the bride.] of my God, the new Jerusalem that descends from heaven; as well as my own new Name. (Emphasis mine)*

---

[9] A continual, habitual victory

Discerning Your Crowns by Speaking in Tongues

When we first started learning about crowns from Ian Clayton, he suggested a way to determine which crowns had been lost was to pray in the spirit until understanding came. We will take that a step or two further to help you identify which crowns have been lost, forfeited, or stolen. We will accomplish this by focused praying in the spirit.

We often do this when we need prayer, but we need discernment to know how best to pray. In this case, we want to focus our praying in the spirit on the subject of crowns—specifically, what crowns we have lost that we need restored to us, and secondly, what crowns we need restored or need to gain.

We know that we can access the Court of Crowns which has (for each of us) a Book of Crowns showing us what we have, what we should have, and what we need restored to us as well as what crowns we have lost and the details about that loss such as when, who was involved, and knowledge of what else may have been lost at that time.

Heaven has more information than we realize about these crowns. You can find out the strategy used to steal your crown or to cause you to forfeit your crown(s).

- Step into the Court of Crowns.

- Ask to see the Registry of Crowns.
- If you are unable to perceive the information on the registry, then
- Focus on praying in the spirit with that in mind for 90 seconds.
- Clarity should be provided regarding lost, forfeited, or stolen crowns.
- Follow the unction of Holy Spirit.
- Request the restoration of the lost crowns(s)
- Place the crown upon your head
- Request the restoration of the authorization of that crown
- Request the release of the complete package of that crown
- Receive the above

The complete package of a crown consists of:

- The Crown
- The Mantle
- The Throne
- The Dominion
- The anointing
- The Glory
- The Scepter
- The Resources

As you pray in the spirit, understanding will often come to your mind through hearing words, phrases, images, or a knowing within you. If needed, follow the first part of your instruction to your spirit, then pray in tongues some more until you get the next instruction. Continue this until your work is complete.

Often feelers or knowers operate by unction, which is defined as the act of anointing with oil. I am referring to the knowing or feeling unmistakable to you and from which you can operate. It is the infusion of anointing to speak or act from one's spirit rather than one's soul.

1 John 2:20:

*But you have an **anointing (unction)** from the Holy One, and you know all things. (Emphasis mine)*

1 John 2:27:

*But the **anointing (unction)** which you have received from Him abides in you, and you do not need that anyone teach you; but as the same **anointing (unction)** teaches you concerning all things, and is true, and is not a lie, and just as it has taught you, you will abide in Him. (Emphasis mine)*

Those who perceive by hearing need not expect an audible voice to speak to them. Instead, it will be a word or a series of words that you must pay attention to.

For those perceiving by seeing, it can manifest as a movie, snapshot, or series of images. Sometimes you hear, and the visual aspect opens to you. However the perception comes, receive it and learn to work with it.

Instructions for the Different Perception Types

Seers

- Step into the Court of Crowns by faith.
- Notice the crowns on the floor or look in your Book of Crowns.
- Ask for insight as to which crown to obtain.
- Pick it up.
- Place it upon your head—if you need to repent of anything, do that first.
- Request the reauthorization of the crown upon your life.
- Request the release of the complete package of that crown.
- Receive it.

Hearers

- Step into the Court of Crowns by faith.
- Open your Book of Crowns.
- Ask angels to read it to you or hear in your spirit what crown to obtain.
- Ask for insight as to which crown to obtain.
- Pick it up.
- Place it upon your head—if you need to repent of anything, do that first.
- Request the reauthorization of the crown upon your life.

- Request the release of the complete package of that crown.
- Receive it.

Knowers

- Step into the Court of Crowns by faith.
- Open your Book of Crowns.
- Ask angels to read it or pay attention to the knowing in your spirit what crown to obtain.
- Ask for insight as to which crown to obtain.
- Pick it up.
- Place it upon your head—if you need to repent of anything, do that first.
- Request the reauthorization of the crown upon your life.
- Request the release of the complete package of that crown.
- Receive it.

Feelers

- Step into the Court of Crowns by faith.
- Open your Book of Crowns.
- Gain a sense of what is in the book within your spirit of what crown to obtain.
- Ask for insight as to which crown to obtain.
- Pick it up.

- Place it upon your head—if you need to repent of anything, do that first.
- Request the reauthorization of the crown upon your life.
- Request the release of the complete package of that crown.
- Receive it.

You may often feel, know, or hear, then begin to see, feel, or know, then start to hear.

Use your sanctified imagination.

Maximizing How You Perceive

- For Knowers: follow your knowing—impressions—you may only know a word
- For Feelers: follow the direction of your feelings
- For Hearers: listen to the word from Heaven.
- For Seers: look for the one that stands out to you

Understanding how you perceive from Heaven is vital. Often, people will compare what they think is a lack of perception with someone who sees very differently. That trap frustrates people and keeps them from exploring and understanding the process. Many times, our abilities to perceive improve with use. We also must not despise how we perceive things because they are unlike so-and-so.

Any golfer knows that they are never playing against other golfers. They are playing the course and the conditions of a particular day. Keep that in mind as you continue your journey of sonship.

———— ∞ ————

Chapter 5

Your Crown of Authority

As we engaged Heaven this day, Ezekiel presented himself. It was as if he were in a movie, and he leaned out of the screen and told us he was part of the storyline.[10]

Stephanie asked, "What is the storyline today?" She began to see a great battle, and she realized it was a cosmic one. They showed her the background. She could see different cosmic dimensions, and Ezekiel stood in front of what we would view as a star, a brightly lit star. He took his sword and pierced it. It was the Bright and Morning Star. As he did so, a liquid poured forth that appeared pure in its form, with gold and white elements flowing out. As it poured out, the star seemed to collapse.

---

[10] This chapter taken from *Embracing Your Crown of Authority* by Dr. Ron M. Horner, LifeSpring Publishing (2025).

Ezekiel moved up to a host of other angels that Stephanie began to see. There were millions and millions of angels. She realized that the liquid pouring from the star was falling onto the Earth and into the crowns on their heads. As the last drops of liquid from the star fell onto the Earth, they covered the entire planet. She could hear a shout that the angels had shouted as they came full force towards the Earth. She could see them piercing the atmosphere as they fought in the heavens. She could see from the perspective on Earth that we, the sons, with these crowns filled with oil—this light and gold—had our hands outstretched, and we were praying and speaking to the atmosphere with authority as if the words we spoke empowered the angels.

"What is this about?" Stephanie inquired.

Lady Wisdom (who had joined us) said, "These crowns are vessels upon your heads. The crowns—they are vessels. Supernatural outpourings go *into* these crowns that are upon your heads. Each one is unique to the individual."

Stephanie commented, "I am seeing that although we may have crowns with the same name, what is poured out to the individual and upon their head, filling this crown, is unique to that individual. Will you give me clarity, Ezekiel, on this picture I am seeing? At the beginning of this engagement, I heard you say, 'Great War.' I thought it was the war before humans were put on the Earth, but it's not."

The Spirit of Wisdom came up beside her and took Stephanie by her left hand.

Stephanie said, "Wisdom, tell me and help me understand what this picture represents."

Wisdom replied, "This is the picture of the uniqueness of each crown. The outpouring and the infilling of Jesus into the crown. Just as unique as the relationship each has with the Trinity, so is the uniqueness of what is poured out to the individual.

A diversity among the crowns exists as well as a diversity of the outpouring.

"If each of you carried the same anointing, there would be no use for the body. Discover what has been poured out. The discovery is in the unique intimacy with the Trinity. Jesus, who has poured himself out, is one piece of this.

What do you carry?

"View this in the aspect of the crown on your head, for we know it is not in and of yourselves, but what He has given. See the perspective from the crown. These are the mysteries that are being unfolded to the sons."

Stephanie remarked, "Wisdom told me to ask, 'What is the uniqueness that I carry in my crown?' You are to ask. So, I asked the Trinity—the Father, Son, and Holy Spirit, 'What is the unique pouring out that you have put in my crown?'"

Stephanie continued, "For me, Holy Spirit told me He has given me a specific flavor of speaking that is unique to the Kingdom, a *unique personalization*. The Father said He's given me *a specific authorization*. Jesus said He's given me *a specific organization*.

"How is it unique for the Kingdom?"

- Pause and ask the Trinity: "What is the unique outpouring that you have for my crown?"
- Pause and ask the Father: "What is the unique authorization of my Crown of Authority?"
- Ask Jesus: "What is the specific organization of my crown?"
- And ask Holy Spirit: "What is the unique personalization of my Crown of Authority?"

[If necessary, pause and pray in the spirit before and after each question. These are some of the mysteries Heaven is revealing in this time.]

Stephanie remarked, "They are showing me the crown on top of my head, which is full of the outpoured liquid, and that as I live, move, and have my being in Jesus, I walk in this authorization, organization, and unique personalization; it spills out of this crown." Do you know how, when you walk with a cup of coffee, it's too full and spills over? It looks like that. This is your Crown of Authority.

"It is because it's not *our* authority. This is a picture OF authority."

Holy Spirit spoke, "The authority in *and from* this crown is unique to each person. **Every person walks in a *specific authority* that is different and unique from others.**"

The authority in and from this crown is what is unique to each person.

Everyone has a Crown of Authority.

It is what is being poured into that crown, be it from hell or Heaven, that is unique to the individual.

What are you making your source to draw from?

"I'm seeing a different picture now of the princes and the powers of this Earth pouring out a vile liquid into the Crowns of Authority of those who walk in darkness," Stephanie noted.

"The reason you have a Crown of Authority from the moment of your birth is because *you are from and out of* the Father," Holy Spirit explained. "You are *from* <u>and</u> *out of* His original creation, uniqueness and design."

---

*You are from and out
of His original creation,
uniqueness, and design.*

Stephanie commented, "I see us as babies with this little crown on our head, and that's what the enemy seeks to defile, this specific Crown of Authority that Christ places on us at birth. We rule and reign."

---

*The enemy seeks to defile
this specific Crown of Authority.*

---

*If the crown can be defiled,
it removes the authority of the sons.*

---

*Satan fears when we walk
with the heavenly anointing
poured into the crown's authority.*

Stephanie added, "That is why I initially saw the picture of us all outside with these crowns on. We were speaking, praising, and walking in authority."

We are a part of changing the Earth.

We are a part of assisting angels. We are a part of it all. We are kings and priests. We can be kings and priests for the Kingdom of Heaven or kings and priests to the kingdom of darkness. Satan fell because he saw us in the future and was extremely upset about it. He was upset that the sons were given more authority than he was.

Hebrews 1:5-6 says:

> [5] *For to which of the angels did He ever say: 'You are my son, today I have begotten you?' And again: 'I will be to him a Father, and he shall be to me a son?'*
>
> [6] *But when He again brings the firstborn into the world, He says: 'Let all the angels of God worship Him.'*

God never gave authority to angels like he gives to sons.

Satan did not like his job placement as lead worshipper in Heaven. He wanted the authority the sons had. That dissatisfaction resulted in the rebellion, where one-third of the angels fell.

What we say in the spiritual realm truly does matter, and it assists the angels in many ways. They have great strength, and they do things, but *we* carry the authority.

Stephanie recalled, "Holy Spirit, for as long as I can remember, since I was little, I've had dreams, or I've heard the enemy's voice say that I have no authority."

Holy Spirit asked, "Were you convinced of that?"

"I think I was."

"Then he succeeded."

Wisdom inquired, "Do you believe you have authority now?"

Stephanie replied, "Yes, yes, I do. I'll take this image with me when ministering to someone, this crown that spills out the Glory, this crown that spills out all of Him! That is a good picture for me and a reminder that nothing is in and of myself, but I do have the Crown of Authority that He has given me, that He is inside of."

Being led to Revelation 3, Stephanie read from the Mirror Bible:

> *² Awake from your slumber. Get a firm grip on what little life you have left in you. Your work does not mirror my finished work. ³ Remember, therefore, what it felt like when you first heard*

and embraced the word as your own. It was like discovering a priceless treasure (like a crown). Now make up your mind once and for all. Why should I surprise you like a thief and break into your space whilst you are fast asleep and not even anticipating my intimate intent; not knowing the moment of my visitation?

⁴ Yet you do have a few individual names in Sardis who have **not forgotten their true identity and soiled their garments.** *They are those* **who walk with me in innocence** *and* **who mirror the reference of their worth to be equal to my estimate of them.** *⁵ Everyone who sees their victory in me, I will clothe in white garments and they will realize that I am not in the business of fulfilling their law and performance based fears by blotting out their names from the Book of Life. Instead, I'm the one who endorses their identity face-to-face before my father and his celestial shepherd messengers."*

⁶ Now listen up with your inner ears. Hear with understanding what the spirit is saying to the ecclesia. ⁷ And to the messenger of the ecclesia of Philadelphia write: I am the holy and true one. I hold the key of David as prophesied in Isaiah 22:22. Yes, I unlock the mysteries of the heavenly dimensions and no one can shut the door and I lock the entrance and none can access it. ⁸ I am fully aware of your efforts in doing the work of the ministry. I want you to see something I have given you a doorway right in front of you that has been fully opened into the heavenly dimensions. Nothing can possibly close it again. Even when you have very little strength, you have treasured my word and have not contradicted my name.

⁹ Behold, the Jewish disguise will be exposed to be the synagogue of Satan. They have sourced their gatherings and accusations, but now I give them to you and will cause them to come face to face with you in fellowship and acknowledgement of my love, which I have bestowed upon you. ¹⁰ You have greatly valued the prophetic word which came to fulfillment in what I endured. I will also guard you with great care, empowering you to stand strong in the midst of the troubled times that are about to come upon the inhabited world to scrutinize the dwellers of the Earth.

¹¹ Do not let tough times make me seem distant from you. I am at hand. See my nearness, not my absence, and don't let temporal setbacks diminish your authority either. ***Remember that you call the shots, you wear the crown. My crown endorses your crown. Let nothing take your crown.*** *He is the king of kings and Lord of lords, not the king of slaves. He redeems* *his life from the pit and weaves the crown for him out of loving and kindness and tender mercies. ¹² It is in your individual continual association with your victory in me that I will make you to be like a strong pillar in the inner shrine of God's sanctuary, supporting the entire structure of my God habitation within you, a place to be your permanent abode from which you will never have to depart. I will engrave upon you the name of my God. Also, I want to know the name of the city of my God, the new Jerusalem that descends from Heaven, and my own new name. And to the celestial shepherd messenger of the Ecclesia, he who speaks is the Amen. He's the ultimate evidence and the one who defines faith. He personifies truth. She is the very source of God's creation.' ¹³ Now listen up with your inner ears. Hear with understanding what the Spirit is saying to the ecclesia. ¹⁴ And to the celestial shepherd-messenger of the ecclesia in Laodicea write: he who speaks in the amen.* ***He is the ultimate evidence and the one who defines faith; he personifies the truth,*** *she (Lady Wisdom) is the very source of God's creation. (MIRROR) (Emphasis and additions mine)*

In Proverbs 8:12-32 we find that Wisdom was at the beginning, at creation:

[12] "I, wisdom, dwell with prudence, and find out knowledge and discretion. [13] The fear of the LORD is to hate evil; pride and arrogance and the evil way and the perverse mouth I hate. [14] Counsel is mine, and sound wisdom; I am understanding, I have strength. [15] By me kings reign, And rulers decree justice. [16] By me princes rule, and nobles, all the judges of the earth. [17] I love those who love me, and those who seek me diligently will find me. [18] Riches and honor are with me, enduring riches and righteousness. [19] My fruit is better than gold, yes, than fine gold, and my revenue than choice silver. [20] I traverse the way of righteousness, in the midst of the paths of justice, [21] That I may cause those who love me to inherit wealth, that I may fill their treasuries.

[22] "The LORD possessed me at the beginning of His way, before His works of old. [23] I have been established from everlasting, from the beginning, before there was ever an earth. [24] When there were no depths I was brought forth, when there were no fountains abounding with water.

[25] Before the mountains were settled, before the hills, I was brought forth; [26] While as yet He had not made the earth or the fields, or the primal dust of the world. [27] **When He prepared the heavens, I was there**, *when He drew a circle on*

the face of the deep, ²⁸ *When He established the clouds above, when He strengthened the fountains of the deep,* ²⁹ *When He assigned to the sea its limit, so that the waters would not transgress His command, when He marked out the foundations of the earth,* ³⁰ ***Then I was beside Him as a master craftsman; and I was daily His delight, rejoicing always before Him,*** ³¹ *Rejoicing in His inhabited world, and my delight was with the sons of men.*

³² *Now therefore, listen to me, my children, for blessed are those who keep my ways. (Emphasis mine)*

For anyone who believes they are too small or have done too much that has been wrong, *the crown came from the Father when He created us* and when we choose to be filled with the goodness of the Bright and Morning Star. With the authority that He has given us, we don't ever have to worry about that again.

I'm excited. As the people begin praying for this, the great mystery of the individual anointing and authority on their life will unfold as they discover what that is.

Stephanie asked, "Ezekiel, what is the picture of what you pierced with your sword?"

Ezekiel replied, "He was pierced for your transgressions."

Isaiah 53:5:

*But he was **pierced for our rebellion (transgression)**, crushed for our sins. He was beaten so we could be whole. He was whipped so we could be healed. (Emphasis mine)*

Stephanie continued, "Yeah, but that's what Ezekiel keeps saying. He was pierced. That's why what he did created this anointing for all the sons."

"This is your original design," Ezekiel noted.

"The picture is not you piercing this," Stephanie commented. "He was pierced, and you are just showing us a picture of what happened on the cross. This is much more profound than what we thought."

Wisdom added, "The pouring out is celestial, is supernatural, it is dimensional, and it's a picture of the unique authorization and filling of our crowns to walk in the authority, boldness and execution of our sonship on this Earth."

Stephanie added, "I saw so many angels when Ezekiel pierced it, and then he went up, and he was with these millions of angels, and they came warring down upon the Earth, fighting the principalities and powers of the air, co-laboring with the ecclesia.

Thank You, Heaven. Thank You, Father, and thank You, Jesus. I ask that for every person that hears this message and they ask for the mystery for themselves, the uniqueness of what You have poured into their Crown of Authority, that they are empowered in their heart and their mind, realizing that this lie that we've all believed— that we have no authority, is dismantled forever.

Thank You, Jesus, that You were poured out and overcame our transgressions so we might walk in the authority as sons. Thank You, Wisdom, for being present from the beginning.

─────── ∞ ───────

Chapter 6
Have You Received Your Mantles?

In an earlier chapter, I listed the typical components packaged with a crown, which include:

- **The Crown** – The obvious representation of the authority you carry in the particular arena your crown encompasses.
- **The Mantle** – Coupled with the Anointing, this is the empowerment of Heaven for what your Crown represents and provides.
- **The Throne** – The seated place of your dominion.
- **The Dominion** – the arena of authority you possess.
- **The Anointing** – that accompanies the crown. It is proof of the authorization of the Crown by Heaven.
- **The Scepter** – symbolizing your throne.
- **The Glory** – the expression of Heaven you carry as you wear your crown.

- **Resources** – To facilitate the anointing and dominion of a crown, certain resources (property, finances, personnel) are allocated by Heaven.

Crowns

It should be evident to us by now what crowns are, but we may not have considered their all-encompassing nature. How important they are to us. And how their absence from our lives can hinder our ability to fulfill our scrolls. Our scrolls contain instructions for our lives.

Mantles

In the natural a mantle is a type of garment. Just like crowns, Mantles need to be picked up and placed upon our shoulders. We have the promise of Jesus that

> ...His yoke is easy, and His burden (mantle) is light.[11]

---

*The enemy is afraid of crowns, but he's **more afraid** of the mantles.*

---

[11] Matthew 11:30

Our enemy does not want to give up ground to us, and as we learn about our rights as sons and understand all Jesus accomplished on our behalf, we will find ourselves in places of greater victory and dominion in our lives. Crowns are not merely an award system, they are an expression of the dominion and mantles that we, as sons, are intended to walk in throughout our lives.

---

*With crowns,
you walk in your authority;
with the mantles,
you assert your authority.*

Mantles are garments representing calling and ability. Elijah had a mantle that denoted the strength he carried.

An example of this is found in 2 Kings 2:1, 8-15:

> *¹ And it came to pass, when the LORD was about to take up Elijah into Heaven by a whirlwind, that Elijah went with Elisha from Gilgal.*
>
> *⁸ Now **Elijah took his mantle, rolled it up**, and **struck the water; and it was divided this way and that, so that the two of them crossed over on dry ground**. ⁹ And so it was, when they had crossed over, that Elijah said to Elisha, 'Ask! What may I do for you, before I am taken away*

from you?' Elisha said, 'Please let a double portion of your spirit be upon me.'

¹⁰ So he said, 'You have asked a hard thing. Nevertheless, if you see me when I am taken from you, it shall be so for you; but if not, it shall not be so.'

*¹¹ Then it happened, as they continued on and talked, that suddenly a chariot of fire appeared with horses of fire, and separated the two of them; and Elijah went up by a whirlwind into Heaven. ¹² And Elisha saw it, and he cried out, 'My father, my father, the chariot of Israel and its horsemen!' So he saw him no more. And he took hold of his own clothes and tore them into two pieces. ¹³ He also **took up the mantle of Elijah that had fallen from him**, and went back and stood by the bank of the Jordan.*

*¹⁴ Then **he took the mantle of Elijah** that had fallen from him, and **struck the water**, and **said, 'Where is the LORD God of Elijah?'** And **when he also had struck the water, it was divided this way and that; and Elisha crossed over.***

¹⁵ Now when the sons of the prophets who were from Jericho saw him, they said, 'The spirit of Elijah rests on Elisha.' And they came to meet him, and bowed to the ground before him. (Emphasis mine)

With Elijah's passing, the prophetic office passed to Elisha, as did the crown and mantle. Elisha wasted no time in validating the office.

With a crown comes a mantle.
When you receive a crown,
you receive its mantle also.

Revelation 3:5:

*Everyone **who sees their victory in me, I will clothe in white garments** [mantles] - and they will realize that I am not in the business of fulfilling their law and performance-based fears by blotting out their names from the Book of Life. Instead, I am the one who endorses their identity face to face before my Father and his celestial shepherd-messengers. (MIRROR) (Emphasis mine)*

We know from John 10:10 that the enemy came to kill, steal, and destroy, and he has sought to destroy the family unit by taking the crowns and the mantles at a very young age, creating accusations and unforgiveness. It has kept humanity from walking in wholeness with authority and the re-establishment of them as sons and daughters.

The first point of contact for a human, as designed by the Father, is through the parent. That is why the enemy has roared like a lion. We must destroy what he has been doing and be empowered to re-establish this in people's lives.

Proverbs 1:8 & 10:

Hear my son, your father's instruction and do not forsake your mother's teaching. Indeed, they are a graceful wreath to your head, **a crown** *and ornaments about your neck. A mantle. (Emphasis mine)*

Now that we know that each crown has a corresponding mantle, we can attach our faith to the reception of not only the crown, the reauthorization of a recovered crown, or the anointing that accompanies that crown and the dominion of it, but also the mantle. The weightiness of some crowns can be explained and attributed to the weightiness of the mantle in some cases.

Dealing with Deficiencies

We must address any deficiencies we have regarding our ability to give and receive love from parents so that we can make the progress Heaven has in mind throughout the rest of our lives. Remember that parents cannot give you what they don't possess themselves. That has been the situation for many of us.

When we engaged Heaven and were taught about mantles, Malcolm, our tutor, spoke of having a chip on our shoulders due to disappointments and disillusionment that we have experienced throughout our lives, particularly concerning parents and caregivers. For some, we need to let our parents or caregivers off the hook.

We also have another arena we must deal with—the possible chip on our shoulder. That chip could be offense or dishonor, among many other things. A definition of this idiom is found in the Merriam-Webster Dictionary:

> *: to have an angry or unpleasant attitude or way of behaving caused by a belief that one has been treated unfairly in the past.*[12]
>
> *Example: He has had a chip on his shoulder ever since he didn't get the promotion he was expecting.*

In the engagement, Malcolm placed a chip on Stephanie's shoulder and knocked it off. He explained that mantles cannot land when we have a chip on our shoulder. We must remove the chips so the mantle can land. Some of that is as simple as forgiving, blessing, and releasing them.

---

[12] Merriam-Webster, "Have a chip on one's shoulder," Accessed February 25, 2025.

With a grin, he placed another chip on her shoulder, which grew into a mantle. She had to take the mantle off her shoulders because of the weight of it.

He explained, "There are mantles to be picked up like crowns. What would you say if the coincidence of a chip being placed on a shoulder at the exact moment a mantle was about to fall was indeed no coincidence?

---

*The enemy is afraid of crowns,
but he's more fearful of the mantles.*

---

*Remember, with crowns,
you walk in your authority,
with the mantles,
you assert your authority.*

Stephanie remarked, "Well, I see this one chip on my shoulder. What do I need to do about it?"

She suddenly knew who this chip represented. Stephanie explained that she keeps going into Heaven and talking to Heaven about this situation. However, Stephanie understood she had a chip on her shoulder regarding this person. She continued, "So, Malcolm, I feel like I've come into Heaven, repented of these things, and forgiven this person. Is there a mantle that needs to be picked up?"

He replied, "Yes, there is, but the chip is still there. *You must deal with the chip first.*"

Stephanie prayed a very private prayer regarding this person, even having compassion towards this person in the end.

She then asked Malcolm: "My question to you, Malcolm, is this: As a child, I was receiving a mantle. What was that mantle?"

"I don't know, pick it up."

Stephanie could see it at her feet, so she reached down, picked it up, and put it on her shoulders.

The Mantle of Receiving Love from Your Parents

She remarked, "This is a Mantle of Receiving Love from Your Parents. Wow! I bet many kids had this one knocked off their shoulders, or it couldn't land."

"There is a special mantle for children to carry. The love that is supposed to be given by the parents is in this mantle," Malcolm explained." With this mantle, you can walk in the assuredness, the surety, and the receiving of the love of a father and of a mother that is healthy and pure. It's a mantle of comfort. Many don't have this mantle, but the Lord restores all."

Stephanie prayed,

Father, I thank You for this mantle and ask to step back in time to when I was to receive this mantle from You. I know it was given to me at birth, too, and I had that mantle. I see that it was on me as a baby, but here it's as if this mantle had outgrown the other one, and the new one was to be established, and I missed it, or it came off my shoulders because of this chip.

[You may need to pause and pray a similar prayer.]

Malcolm explained, "Think about this. This mantle is being hindered from landing because of a chip on your shoulder. Maintaining a mantle of a parent's love and comfort would be difficult if you no longer trust it. Let it be reestablished in you. With it will come the comfort and the love—a reestablishment of that parental love."

Stephanie said to Malcolm. "I was just thinking about all the children whose parents gave them away.

"Yes, they are missing this mantle."

"Can you tell me why this mantle is important now that we're adults?"

"Without this mantle, *receiving love from anyone is very difficult.* Many hold others at arm's length. Many have difficulty being a parent and refuse the Father's love. So have it reestablished, and reestablishment shall come," Malcolm answered.

"Is this like how, when we walk into the Court of Crowns, there is a reestablishment of the authority of crowns? Is there a particular court?" Stephanie asked.

He replied, "With a crown comes a mantle. When you receive a crown, you are not only receiving a crown, but also its mantle."

Remember:

---
*With a crown comes a mantle.
When you receive a crown,
not only are you receiving a crown,
you are receiving its mantle.*

Stephanie prayed:

I ask to step into the Court of Crowns to receive my Crown of Parental Love and Comfort, my mantle, and the authority that comes with it to be reestablished into my life.

Stephanie asked, "Malcolm, how does this work for those who were adopted or whose parents may have let them live with them, but they abuse them?"

"It is the same," he replied. "This is for their healing. This is for their reestablishment and feeling like human beings, feeling love.

Stephanie remarked, "We cannot do this without forgiving all who have deeply wounded us. That is why we cannot have a chip on our shoulders when we come here.

Father, I pray that many will be reestablished into wholeness from this mantle being placed back on the shoulders and this Crown of Nurture and Being Nurtured.

"Malcolm, I want to be sure of the name of this. I see its value, especially for so many who lost a parent in childbirth, whose parents gave them away, or who lived in abusive, horrific situations where the reality was supposed to be their first understanding of love through a parent.

"This feels like a wrap-around love. That is what this feels like."

Psalms 32:10:

> *But when you trust in the Lord for forgiveness,* **his wrap-around love will surround you.** *(TPT) (Emphasis mine)*

Psalms 61:3:

> *Lord, You are a paradise of protection to me. You lift me high above the fray. None of my foes can touch me when* **I'm held firmly in your wrap-around presence!** *(TPT) (Emphasis mine)*

People often say, "I know he loves me, but I can't experience it." *That is a mantle that has been lost.* This crown is gone because we are supposed to give our children the picture of the Father's love in an unconditional, loving manner towards a newborn and children.

Thank You, Father, for this crown and this mantle. I know many mantles will coincide with the crowns we receive. I ask for an establishment of all mantles for the crowns I've received to date to be placed upon my shoulder in this wrap-around love that I feel here in this court—the authority that it gives us and the reestablishment. I forgive those in my life who failed to nurture and care for me. I bless them and release them now, in Jesus' name.

Thank You, Your Honor.

Stephanie added, "He's showing me that I see a layer of my mantle and place it around my mom. Because I received it, I can give it. Like Peter and John in the Book of Acts, they said, 'Silver and gold, I don't have, but what I do have, I give to you.'"

I give you this because I know you missed out on this, too. I ask for her to have a Crown of Nurture put back on her head.

[You may want to pray a similar prayer for your parents or caregivers.]

Stephanie remarked, "I feel like the next piece of this will be reestablishing our thrones.

Colossians 3:21 says:

Fathers do not provoke your children lest they become discouraged.

Or, as one translation says:

And fathers, don't have unrealistic expectations for your children or else they may become discouraged. (TPT)

2 Timothy 1:5:

For I am mindful of the sincere faith within you, which first dwelt in your grandmother Lois and your mother Eunice, and I'm sure that is in you as well.

Proverbs 1:8 & 10:

*'Hear my son, your father's instruction and do not forsake your mother's teaching. Indeed, they are a graceful wreath to your head, **a crown** and ornaments about your neck. A mantle.' (Emphasis mine)*

1 Thessalonians 2:7 & 12:

*But we proved to be gentle among you **as a nursing mother, tenderly caring for her own children.** Having so fond an affection for you, we were well pleased to impart to you not only the gospel of God, but also our own lives. (Emphasis mine)*

Stephanie prayed:

Thank You, Lord, for this crown and this mantle that You are reestablishing how I can receive love from You, from Heaven, and how I can be healed from childhood wounds and chips on my shoulders so that the mantles can fall upon me properly.

Help me better understand the mantles that come with crowns and the ones on the ground that I need to retrieve. Give us insight; give us instruction. Open the eyes of my understanding.

As mentioned earlier, receiving these crowns is essential to giving and receiving love adequately. They help provide us with a foundation for later in life. Where we missed this, where these crowns might have been lost or stolen, step back into the Court of Crowns and request their restoration in your life.

Ask for the amendment of "As if it Never Were" and step into the newness of your life, having been loved and now being able to receive and give love.

False Mantles

Many don't recognize that just as you can receive godly mantles into your life, false crowns will manifest false mantles, causing you to exhibit the wrong things.

> *Just as godly crowns have mantles, so do false crowns and ungodly crowns.*

We want their removal. When you recognize you have received a false crown, simply repent and request the removal of the false crown and any false mantle you may have received. Don't live under the expression of ANY false crown. It's time to step into who you truly are, not a counterfeit version your enemy has sought to impose on your life. You have a place of rest from which to begin to operate. It's time to take a seat.

------ ∞ ------

Chapter 7

Are You Seated on Your Throne?

We had just finished our engagement with Heaven concerning mantles when Stephanie remarked, "I feel like the next piece of this will be the reestablishment of our thrones." As part of the packaging of a crown, we must understand that we rule from *a seated place—a throne*. A throne is a heavenly seat from which we exercise the dominion given us as sons. We also must understand what Satan is after in trying to destroy you. He doesn't like you, so he will attack you to get at the Father. Let's read about his demise in Isaiah 14:9-23 where the Father is speaking to Lucifer:

> *⁹ Hell from beneath is excited about you, to meet you at your coming; it stirs up the dead for you, all the chief ones of the earth; it has raised up from their thrones all the kings of the nations.*

10 They all shall speak and say to you: 'Have you also become as weak as we? Have you become like us?

*11 Your **pomp** is brought down to Sheol, and the sound of your stringed instruments; the maggot is spread under you, and worms cover you.'*

12 'How you are fallen from Heaven, O Lucifer, son of the morning! How you are cut down to the ground, you who weakened the nations! 13 For you have said in your heart: 'I will ascend into Heaven, I will exalt my throne above the stars of God; I will also sit on the mount of the congregation on the farthest sides of the north; 14 I will ascend above the heights of the clouds, I will be like the Most High.' 15 Yet you shall be brought down to Sheol, to the lowest depths of the Pit.

16 'Those who see you will gaze at you, and consider you, saying: 'Is this the man who made the earth tremble, who shook kingdoms, 17 who made the world as a wilderness and destroyed its cities, who did not open the house of his prisoners?'

18 'All the kings of the nations, all of them, sleep in glory, everyone in his own house; 19 But you are cast out of your grave like an abominable branch, like the garment of those who are slain, thrust through with a sword, who go down to the stones of the pit, like a corpse trodden underfoot.

²⁰ You will not be joined with them in burial, because you have destroyed your land and slain your people. The brood of evildoers shall never be named.

²¹ Prepare slaughter for his children because of the iniquity of their fathers, lest they rise up and possess the land, and fill the face of the world with cities.'

²² 'For I will rise up against them,' says the LORD of hosts, 'and cut off from Babylon the name and remnant, and offspring and posterity,' says the LORD.

²³ 'I will also make it a possession for the porcupine, and marshes of muddy water; I will sweep it with the broom of destruction,' says the LORD of hosts. (Emphasis mine)

His demise was not going to be desirable. You can see that he lost his crown and then his mantle (he was designed to worship but lifted himself to his destruction). He lost his place in Heaven, and since he lost his crown, throne, and place of dominion, he decided to go after yours. He seeks to steal your crowns. He understands that:

To de-crown you is to dethrone you.

> *To dethrone you is to minimize your placement and your destiny.*

Once you are de-crowned, you are de-throned. The purpose of this is to minimize your impact on the Earth. **Your authority is then given to another.**

Heaven told us that understanding your loss of crowns has been the first step, and retrieving them was next; however, understanding the authority of the crowns is a true revelation. That is why we are discussing the packaging of a crown and all that it entails so that you can maximize your sonship.

> *Understanding the authority of the crowns is true revelation.*

Stephanie remarked, "Do you know what I am seeing? I saw an actual movie after I opened the doors to see when Satan fell.

In Luke 10:18, we read:

And He (Jesus) said to them, 'I saw Satan fall like lightning from Heaven.'

The first thing that was removed from him was his crown before he was thrown out of Heaven (which we just read about), and that's why he seeks ours. Not only does he **steal our crowns**, but *he also wears them* *because they have given him authority over us and our situations in those moments.* **The loss you feel when your crowns are removed is the perpetual state in which he exists.**

---
*The removal of his crown
has caused him to lust after the sons
and the authority of the crowns
that they wear.*

---
*The crowns that we have lost
or forfeited, represent the authority
we have also lost and the thrones
we have forfeited.*

Crowns are a vitally important part of our walk.

---
*The more crowns you remove
from Satan's kingdom
and take back as sons,
the less authority he will have.*

In 1 Peter 5, we read how the enemy seeks those whom He may devour (v. 8). We have always been taught that he seeks to destroy us through sin and temptation. However, the context is that he is seeking to de-crown us so he can de-throne us.

---
*Satan seeks to de-crown us
so he can de-throne us.*
---

1 Peter 5:1-11:

> *¹ The elders who are among you I exhort, I who am a fellow elder and a witness of the sufferings of Christ, and also a partaker of the glory that will be revealed:*
>
> *² Shepherd the flock of God which is among you, serving as overseers, not by compulsion but willingly, not for dishonest gain but eagerly; ³ nor as being lords over those entrusted to you, but being examples to the flock; ⁴ and when the Chief Shepherd appears, you will **receive the crown of glory** that does not fade away. (Emphasis mine)*

Peter is not speaking of a rapture event. He is speaking of when Jesus is unveiled in you as you fully embrace your sonship. We will jointly be partaking in the Glory that will be revealed when we, as sons, embrace our sonship. Glory is part of the package.

> *⁵ Likewise, you younger people, submit yourselves to your elders. Yes, all of you be submissive to one another and be clothed with humility, for 'God resists the proud, but gives grace to the humble.'*

⁶ Therefore humble yourselves under the mighty hand of God, that He may exalt you in due time, ⁷ casting all your care upon Him, for He cares for you.

*⁸ Be sober, be vigilant; because your adversary, the devil, walks about like a roaring lion, **seeking whom he may devour** [seeking whose crown he can steal]. ⁹ Resist him, steadfast in the faith, [with your crown firmly seated on your head] knowing that the same sufferings (affections) are experienced by your brotherhood in the world. ¹⁰ But may the God of all grace, who called us to His eternal glory by Christ Jesus, after you have suffered (felt His passion) a while, perfect, establish, strengthen, and settle you. ¹¹ To Him be the glory and the **dominion** forever and ever. Amen. (Emphasis mine)*

We will talk about dominions in the next chapter.

Zechariah 6:11-14, we read:

*¹¹ Take the silver and gold, make **an elaborate crown**, and set it on the head of Joshua the son of Jehozadak, the high priest. ¹² Then speak to him, saying, 'Thus says the LORD of hosts, saying: 'Behold, the Man whose name is the BRANCH! From His place He shall branch out, and He shall build the temple of the LORD;*

13 Yes, He shall build the temple of the LORD. **He shall <u>bear the glory</u>, and <u>shall sit and rule on His throne</u>; so <u>He shall be a priest on His throne</u>,** *and the counsel of peace shall be between them both.' 14 'Now the elaborate crown shall be for a memorial in the temple of the LORD for Helem, Tobijah, Jedaiah, and Hen the son of Zephaniah.' (Emphasis mine)*

Joshua, the High Priest, had been elevated due to his stewardship of his office, as discussed in Zechariah 3:7.

Stewardship positions you for promotion.

Revelation 4:4:

*Around the throne were **twenty-four thrones, and on the thrones I saw twenty-four elders sitting**, clothed in white robes; and they had **crowns of gold** on their heads. (Emphasis mine)*

In Revelation 4:10-11, we see that the twenty-four elders not only had crowns but also thrones...places from which they ruled.

*10 ...the twenty-four elders fall down before Him **who sits on the throne** and worship Him who lives forever and ever, and **cast their crowns before the throne**, saying: 11 'You are worthy, O Lord, to receive glory and honor and power; for*

You created all things, and by Your will they exist and were created.' (Emphasis mine)

Thrones operate best
from a seat of rest.

YOU operate best from a seat of rest.

Because Jesus now operates from a seat of rest, we can too! A throne is where one sits, which is a resting position.

We govern best from rest.

Hebrews 1:1-3:

> *[1] God, who at various times and in various ways spoke in time past to the fathers by the prophets, [2] has in these last days spoken to us by His Son, whom He has appointed heir of all things, through whom also He made the worlds; [3] who being the brightness of His glory and the express image of His person, and upholding all things by the word of His power, when He had by Himself purged our sins, **sat down at the right hand of the Majesty on high**.... (Emphasis mine)*

These thrones aren't for angels, according to Hebrews 1:13:

> *But to which of the angels has He ever said: 'Sit at my right hand, till I make your enemies your footstool'?*

In Hebrews 2:7, we are told that he has set the son of man over creation and delivered it into our hands to perform.

The Apostle Paul explains how this works in Ephesians 1:15-23:

> [15] *Therefore I also, after I heard of your faith in the Lord Jesus and your love for all the saints,* [16] *do not cease to give thanks for you, making mention of you in my prayers:* [17] *that the God of our Lord Jesus Christ, the Father of glory, may give to you the spirit of wisdom and revelation in the knowledge of Him,* [18] *the eyes of your understanding being enlightened; that you may know what is the hope of His calling, what are the riches of the glory of His inheritance in the saints,* [19] *and what is the exceeding greatness of His power toward us who believe, according to the working of His mighty power* [20] **which He worked in Christ when He raised Him from the dead and <u>seated Him</u> at His right hand in the heavenly places,** [21] *far above all principality and power and might and dominion, and every name that is named, not only in this age but also in that which is to come.* [22] *And He put all things under His feet, and gave Him to be head over all things to the church,* [23] *which is His*

body, the fullness of Him who fills all in all. (Emphasis mine)

Since Jesus is now in a position of rest, we can do the same. The rest is available to us.

Hebrews 4:9-11:

*⁹ There remains therefore a rest for the people of God. ¹⁰ For **he who has entered His rest [his governmental position] has** himself also **ceased from his works** as God did from His. ¹¹ Let us therefore **be diligent to enter that rest**, lest anyone fall according to the same example of disobedience. (Emphasis mine)*

The paradox of Heaven
is that resting
is your governmental position.

We rule from a place of rest, not a place of doing and striving. The throne represents that you have a positional place in the realms of Heaven from which you govern the jurisdiction given to you by Heaven through your crown.

Ephesians 2:4-6:

⁴ But God, who is rich in mercy, because of His great love with which He loved us, ⁵ even when we were dead in trespasses, made us alive together with Christ (by grace you have been *saved), ⁶ and raised us up together, and **made us sit together in the heavenly places in Christ Jesus,** ⁷ that in the ages to come He might show the exceeding riches of His grace in His kindness toward us in Christ Jesus. (Emphasis mine)*

Remember, we read about Lucifer's demise when he rebelled in Isaiah 14:13:

*For you have said in your heart: 'I will ascend into Heaven, I will exalt **my throne** above the stars of God; I will also **sit on the mount** of the congregation On the farthest sides of the north....*

---

*Satan wanted
what was reserved for the sons.*

---

*As sons step into their rightful place,
they will be able to extend the rule
of the Kingdom of Heaven
to the Earth realm.*

That is the purpose of our crowns and thrones.

Colossians 1:16:

For by Him all things were created that are in heaven and that are on earth, visible and invisible, whether **thrones** *or* **dominions** *or principalities or powers. All things were created through Him and for Him. (Emphasis mine)*

---

*Sons rule best when
they rule from a place of rest.*

As we stepped into the Library again, Stephanie noticed a book on the bookcase that was pulled out slightly. Being led to the bookcase, she picked up *The Book of Thrones*. We had asked to know what Heaven had to say about thrones. On the cover was a massive lion at the foot of a throne. A woman was also standing nearby. The woman reached over and opened the book for Stephanie. It was Mary Magdalene with whom we had engaged before.

Looking at the book, Stephanie could see the words *The Throne*. "I am placing my fingers on this page and the words, *The Throne*." She saw the image of what she perceived as the throne on which the Ancient of Days sits.

She understood that every throne created came from that throne, as if it had been whittled out of its frame. Whatever that throne is made of, every throne has come from it. She could feel pieces of it in her fingers as if they were pieces of gold. Their edges were sharp, and it was very hard. When she felt around the page, she could see diamonds. She picked up pieces of diamonds and flakes of gold that were all over the page.

Mary Magdalene explained,

Thrones are your seat of authority.

You <u>wear</u> the crowns.
You <u>have</u> a seat.

"Each seat is a unique design."

Within the throne, Stephanie could see the movement of water within. Stephanie asked, "What is the water?"

Mary Magdalene explained, "This is where deep calls to deep."

Stephanie remarked, "I'm beginning to realize that in every throne, there are elements the Father has put in. He has placed within each throne a wonder, evoking awe and wonder, life and reflections of His Majesty. I see a reflection in a mirror and hear the words, "A Grounding," the force that keeps this grounded, and I see the blood. I saw fire.

"We've seen things that are hot in the natural, so hot, so molten that you can see the burning around the figure. It's like a wave coming off something that's extremely hot. It's not that I'm seeing flames of fire, but I know that this throne is hot."

She asked Mary Magdalene, "Are individual thrones created from the main throne?" Is that what our thrones are filled with?"

She immediately had an image of millions and millions of tiny thrones coming into His throne. She could see where each throne was carved out of the piece of His throne. She could see our thrones going *back to* their original design from THE Throne.

Stephanie said, "Mary, we have been so deceived that we didn't have any authority. The thrones I see come from His throne, which we occupy, and are intricately carved. We have been deceived into believing we did not have a seat of authority. We were deceived that we weren't or aren't seated in Heavenly places with Him.

"You want to show us that everything came out of this throne that the Father sits on—the Great I Am. It's as if this throne *is* His mind."

Mary Magdalene asked, "Now, can you picture being seated *with* Him?"

"I can."

"Now, can you see being seated *in* Him?"

"Yes."

"Now, can you see that you are *from* Him? This is identity. This is true identity—identify that you are formed *from* Him."

---
*From His throne,
He created you <u>and</u> your throne.*

Luke 17:20-21:

The Pharisee demanded to know from him. So when do you say the kingdom of God would finally arrive? He answered them. God's kingdom does not arrive as a reward for someone's scrupulous scrutiny. It's neither here nor there. Look and see for yourselves. It is closer to you than what you ever imagined. The kingdom of God is within you. (MIRROR)

Luke 17:22:

All things were endowed on me by my Father. No one knows the son like the Father does and it is not possible to know the Father unless the son, who knows him intimately, unveils him to the one who wishes to see him. **The only possible way to really <u>know the son</u> is through the Father's eyes - and the <u>only possible way to really know the Father is through the eyes of sonship!</u>** *(The only way to really know who you are, is to discover yourself through the Father's eyes! This unveiling doesn't happen through mere academic or philosophical scrutiny.) (MIRROR) (Emphasis Mine)*

The only way to really know who you are is to discover yourself through the Father's eyes. That this unveiling doesn't happen through mere academic or philosophical scrutiny. And some will start pointing you to various locations of their imagination. Don't go there for just like a flash of lightning can eliminate the sky in a moment. So is the unveiling of the son of man.

Stephanie said, "They keep taking me to Luke 17:3:

Mirrored in your own eyes. Remind your brother of his value....

"It's our purpose to remind them of their value that they were cut from this incredible throne of God and have that Crown of Authority."

She asked, "Mary Magdalene, why are you our teacher? What is it that the Lord is redeeming or has redeemed in you for you to be our teacher about thrones?"

Mary Magdalene replied, "I am the one that washed His feet."

"Identity. It's about identity. She's so gentle. Thank you. Mary Magdalene.

"I realize that every time I sit down in this place (the Library of Revelation), it's not a regular chair I sit on. As I looked around, I realized there were crowns everywhere. I'm wondering if Heaven will help me as we step in here, and I see crowns in position in different places, that if we are to learn about a crown, we can go over to it, pick it up, and learn or ask about it. I see that each crown represents a mantle," Stephanie described.

Mary Magdalene remarked, "You either get a mantle or a millstone."

With that, Stephanie replied, "Wow."

———— ∞ ————

Chapter 8
Have You Exercised Your Dominion?

Now that we know that each crown has a corresponding mantle, and we have attached our faith to the reception of the crown, the mantle, and the throne, now let's understand a bit about the dominion that is a part of the package of a crown. We have received the reauthorization of a recovered crown—or the commissioning of a new one—along with the mantle that accompanies it and the dominion it carries. The weightiness of some crowns can be explained and attributed to the weightiness of the mantle in some cases. Still, it can also be attributed to the weightiness of the dominion that specific crown encompasses.

A dominion could be geographical or to a particular arena, such as a specific business arena. It could be to a particular musical style or a specific niche that you can bring kingdom change to. We often think of dominions as geographical and it is easier for us to picture this in our minds. One might have dominion over a city, or a part of a city, or within a subculture within that city. Any number of possibilities exist.

The Apostle Paul wrote in Colossians 1:16:

> *For by Him all things were created that are in heaven and that are on earth, visible and invisible, whether thrones or **dominions** or principalities or powers. All things were created through Him and for Him. (Emphasis mine)*

Since God was the original Creator, He is simply exercising His original dominion and bringing back creation under His care through His sons.

The original instruction to Adam is found in Genesis 1:27-31:

> [27] *So God created man in His own image; in the image of God He created him; male and female He created them.*
>
> [28] *Then God blessed them, and God said to them, 'Be fruitful and multiply; fill the earth and subdue it;* **have dominion** *over the fish of the sea, over the birds of the air, and over every living thing that moves on the earth.'*
>
> [29] *And God said, 'See, I have given you every herb that yields seed which is on the face of all the*

earth, and every tree whose fruit yields seed; to you it shall be for food.

³⁰ Also, to every beast of the earth, to every bird of the air, and to everything that creeps on the earth, in which there is life, I have given every green herb for food'; and it was so.

³¹ Then God saw everything that He had made, and indeed it was very good. So the evening and the morning were the sixth day. (Emphasis mine)

Dominion originally given to Adam was forfeited by his disobedience in eating of the Tree of the Knowledge of Good and Evil. Jesus came and fulfilled the requirements to restore dominion to the sons. The restoration is coming as we embrace the crowns designed by Heaven for us to wear.

Heaven said to us:

The sun is rising on new technologies and advancements for the sons on behalf of the Kingdom of Heaven. These are territorial advancements. There are crowns and thrones, dominions and authority that are purposed in this sun that is rising upon the sons.

Specific technologies
are in the crowns.

> *Purpose and dominion*
> *are on the thrones (and in them).*

These are technologies that are superior and everlasting. With every new sunrise, there is dominion, technologies, and authority the sons must take.

> *The crowns are key,*
> *and **every** crown has*
> *an associated throne and dominion.*

There is a purpose to the new day, and *you must govern the whispers.*

> *In governing the whispers*
> *with these crowns and technologies,*
> *authority, and dominion,*
> *you will pull down strongholds—*
> *ancient ones.*

This is a new day!

We asked, "What do we need to do?"

Malcolm and Einstein appeared as our teachers, and Einstein said, "This is my favorite part of the technologies of Heaven. They have been engrafted into each crown using a very interesting code.

> *There is an encoding on the crowns specific to that crown.*

For instance, with the Crown of Sonship, we are to incorporate the technologies of the crown into the words that we speak for the new day, the new dominion, and our new authority. There is a formula for each crown. Ask Heaven to help you.

I thank You, Father, for this new day and for the Crown of Sonship—the authority and dominion You have given me as a son and the technologies, and the Crown of All Things New.

I bless the Earth with the dominion You've given the sons. This is the day the Lord has made; we will rejoice and be glad.

I co-labor with the angels and walk in the dominion and the authority with which the crown has given me, and I speak life, not death.

I declare the dominion and authority of Jesus, who makes all things new, tearing down the enemy's strongholds, collaborating with the angels as kings and priests as I celebrate the new day.

We could see Einstein blessing the Earth and showing us this dominion and authority over the Earth,

Thank You, Lord, for making all things new—even the Earth—this day. Thank You for the technologies of

Heaven, the dominion, and the authority that You give the sons.

I bless the Earth and its fullness, which belongs to You.

I kept thinking that we would do something profound, but this is the simplicity of blessing the Earth, and our dominion and authority, and it transpires while we do this.

Colossians 1:16:

*Everything that is, begins in him; whether in the heavenly realm or upon the earth, visible or invisible, he is the original blueprint of every order of justice and every level of authority, **be it kingdoms or governments, principalities or jurisdictions;** the original form of all things were founded by him and created for him. (MIRROR) (Emphasis mine)*

Or,

*For by Him all things were created that are in heaven and that are on earth, visible and invisible, whether **thrones or dominions** or principalities or powers. All things were created through Him and for Him. (Emphasis mine)*

The Mirror Bible translates 'dominion' as 'government' in the passage above. Your crown represents a government, and you are to govern that government according to the instructions of Heaven.

In Colossians 1:20:

*He initiated the reconciliation of all things to himself. Through the blood of the cross **God restored the original harmony. His reign of peace now extends to every visible thing upon the earth as well as those invisible things which are in the heavenly realm.** (Emphasis mine)*

Isaiah 9:6-7:

*⁶ For unto us a Child is born, unto us a Son is given; And **the government will be upon His shoulder.** And His name will be called Wonderful, Counselor, Mighty God, Everlasting Father, Prince of Peace.*

*⁷ **Of the increase of His government and peace** There will be no end, Upon the throne of David and over His kingdom, To **order it** and **establish it** with **judgment** and **justice** from that time forward, even forever. The zeal of the Lord of hosts will perform this.*

---

*Blessing the Earth
is expressing dominion.*

When we do so, there is something very transformative about what we do. Still, we can't do it appropriately or conduct this appropriately without the crowns because we must understand...

> *The authority we have*
> *is because of the crowns.*

> *Technologies are upon each crown,*
> *encoded into each crown,*
> *and embedded in*
> *the corresponding dominion.*

> *Each crown has a different*
> *coding unique to the wearer.*

It is different and unique to each person.

As we follow Heaven's instructions and commands in exercising this dominion, and we verbally bless the Earth, transformational things will occur.

As you have been told, the act of vocally blessing the Earth is an extension and operation of your dominion upon the Earth. Many have settled for an elementary understanding of these things, but the Father doesn't want us to settle for elementary things. He wants us to branch out and begin possessing the land. As I was learning about crowns and dominions, the Father said the following. Notice how much He spoke of dominion:

> *Many talk about the wealth of the sinner being laid up for the just, but they expect it will simply*

fall into their lap. Some may, but most require the trade of labor and energy which you possess as a son. Don't fall for the tricks and traps of everything being entirely easy. You must press into some of these things to see them manifest. I have things for my sons to do, but they have been timid about pursuing them and have pushed these thoughts down and into the backs of their minds. I'm bringing them up again. I am bringing the desire to walk in **greater dominion** *into your life. Many crowns have current applications for the sons and need to be implemented.* **Understand that dominion is for now,** *not hundreds of years from now.*

In Psalm 8, you are **given dominion**. *Jesus enforced it before his ascension, and I have not changed My mind.* **Because Jesus has authority, YOU have authority.** *Because of that imparted authority, you go and preach. You go and make disciples of ALL nations. You baptize them into the nature of the Father, Son, and Holy Spirit.*

Hebrews 2:8:

God's intention was that human life should rule the planet. He **subjected everything without exception to his control.** *Yet, looking at the human race, it does not seem that way at all. (MIRROR) (Emphasis mine)*

> *Understand that because*
> *I have a crown, **you** have a crown.*
> *Because I have dominion,*
> *YOU have dominion.*

That's what it means to be coronated.

We have learned that crowns represent dominions, and with a crown comes the authorization to exercise Kingdom authority within that dominion.

Crowns Represent Dominions

When we understand that crowns represent dominions or areas of dominion, we begin to grasp the importance of obtaining crowns, regaining lost, stolen, or forfeited crowns, maintaining our crowns, and ultimately maximizing our crowns.

You may have once conquered an area of your life and received a crown related to that victory. However, somewhere along the way, that crown may have been lost—whether through your own actions or the actions of others.

There may have been a time when your zeal for the Father burned far stronger than it does today. Did something happen to cause that zeal to wane? Chances are, someone stole your Crown of Zeal—or you surrendered it. And when that crown was taken, the strength and anointing that accompanied it also lifted from your life.

Do you remember the joy and energy you had before losing that crown? Don't you want it back?

Satan does not want you to have, maintain, or walk in the dominion that your crown represents. He works to orchestrate the capture of your crowns, knowing that if he succeeds, he strips away your authority in areas where you once walked in victory and strength.

If there is an area of your life where you once stood firm but now feel weakened, it's a sign that you have lost that crown—and with it, the strength it carried.

Court Scenario

Let's pray:

I ask for access to the Court of Crowns.

Father, where I messed up, I repent.

Where I allowed others to steal my crowns or knock them off my head, I repent.

Where I allowed Satan to steal my crown(s) and did not resist him, I repent.

Where I laid my crown down or knocked it off my head myself, I repent.

I forgive, bless, and release those involved in losing my crown(s).

I ask angels to go to the trophy rooms of hell and retrieve my crowns.

Where my crowns have been profaned, I ask that the blood of Jesus would cleanse them.

Where I have despised a crown, I repent.

Where I have chosen not to walk in the authority of my crown(s), I repent.

I ask your forgiveness for all these areas where I messed up. Thank you for forgiveness, in Jesus' name.

In this Court of Crowns, I ask angels to assist me and show me which crowns to retrieve today.

I receive this Crown of _____ today.

I ask for the re-authorization of this crown for my life.

I receive the re-authorization of this crown now.

I receive the release of the mantle, the throne, the dominion, the scepter, the anointing, the Glory, and the resources of this crown into my life.

Thank you, Father.

*Crowns are an expression
of dominion.*

*Once Satan obtains a crown
from a son, he wears it to confiscate
the dominion it represents.*

To understand that each crown represents an area of one's life in which one has experienced victory is to understand that it is one less area the enemy must confront you successfully in. Also, when you achieve victory in an area, you are then empowered to teach others how to achieve victory in that same area. Thus reducing Satan's dominion in people's lives.

*Once you receive a particular crown,
he may attempt to steal it from you,
but you can learn to walk in a grace
that makes his attempts futile
against your life.*

You want to be aware of attempts by the enemy to steal your crowns from you. Confrontations are often attempts to steal a crown. Don't take the bait.

Father wants us to be victorious in battle and obtain the spoils of that battle, including the dominion that the captured crowns represent.

Commission your angels to make you aware quickly of attempts to steal your crown.

I call my angels near.

[When you sense their nearness, say:]

I commission you to make me aware when attempts are made to steal my crown, whether from people, principalities or powers, LHSs, demons, or Satan—from whomever.

Thank you for your diligence in this matter as we co-labor together.

If you have ever harbored unforgiveness and have repented, realize that forgiveness creates one less area of dominion that Satan once possessed.

---
*The more we forgive,
the less dominion he has.*

---
*More areas of freedom
result in fewer areas
of the dominion of Satan.*

In an earlier journaling, the Father said this:

More understanding is coming for the Crown's book. As you keep digging, revelation will *unfold. I have much to share with My sons on the subject. I want them to understand the crowns and **the dominion they possess as sons**. It is not just a cute concept but a life-changing one for those who embrace what I'm doing in this day and hour.*

---
*Crowns are critical
for the sons to understand.*

Each of the kings who chose to fight against Joshua lost their crowns, their dominion, and their place of authority.

Each crown designates a place of dominion. Joshua was operating under a dominion that included the entire land of Canaan. What is your place of dominion?

---
*It is not just a loss of a crown,
it is an expression of the dominion
of that crown.*

Stand in the authority the crown represents and take dominion where you are placed. The time is NOW!

———— ∞ ————

Chapter 9
Have You Embraced Your Anointing?

As we learn more about the package the crown contains, we need to understand that crowns also contain anointings from which we function under the authority of a specific crown. We all possess an anointing that comes from the Crown of Righteousness that is ours because we have given our lives to Jesus, and all have been given a Crown of Authority. Whether that is maximized or not is another matter.

The anointing accompanying a crown releases freedom and boldness to express what Heaven has for you to say in a specific arena. Those who typically are timid have the strength and fortitude to speak and declare boldly the truth of Heaven about a manner. This could be in any kind of setting. It is not reserved just for church settings. It may express itself in boldness to speak to a total stranger or close friend when prompted by the Holy Spirit.

---

*Satan fears when we walk
with the heavenly anointing
that is poured into
the crown's authority.*

Crowns Represent Anointings

When we understand that crowns contain mantles, thrones, or areas of dominion, the Glory of God, and more, we need boldness to operate. That is where the anointing comes in.

Isaiah 10:27:

> *In that day, the Lord will remove the heavy burden from your shoulders and break off the yoke of bondage from your necks **because of the heavy anointing upon you.** (TPT) (Emphasis mine)*

As we can begin to fathom the importance of obtaining crowns, whether lost, stolen, or forfeited, and the further significance of maintaining our crowns, we will experience and witness the expansion of the Kingdom of Heaven upon the Earth.

Satan does not want you to have or maintain that dominion that the crown represents, and he certainly does not wish for you to operate in the anointing it brings into your life. He will try to orchestrate a capturing of that crown from your life, and if he is successful, he will then have removed your authority in that area of your life and the accompanying anointing. With the capturing of that crown, the accompanying aspects of that crown are also forfeited.

We are instructed to catch the foxes that would spoil the vines. These foxes seek to steal the crown from your head—the anointing and authority you carry that you are to produce change in the Earth with. Tender grapes are not quite ready for harvest and need protection from those who would impact their life by premature destruction. From the crushing of grapes comes sweet wine.

Song of Solomon 2:15:

Catch us the foxes, the little foxes that spoil the vines, for our vines have tender grapes.

Lingering human spirits can be assigned to orchestrate the stealing of your crowns. We must be aware that Satan uses any tactic he can to fulfill his purposes, and no, he doesn't play fair.

There are characteristics of crowns that each of us carry. It is a type of mantle in many respects and expresses itself through a particular anointing.

> *Just as mantles
> represent anointings,
> so do crowns.*

> *The anointing is an empowerment.*

Speaking to Elijah, the Lord, 1 Kings 19:15-16, said:

*¹⁵ Then the LORD said to him: 'Go, return on your way to the Wilderness of Damascus; and when you arrive, **anoint Hazael as king over Syria.'** ¹⁶ 'Also, you shall **anoint Jehu the son of Nimshi as king over Israel**. And Elisha the son of Shaphat of Abel Meholah, you shall anoint as prophet in your place.'*

In Old Testament times, when someone was anointed for a task, the prophet or priest would pour oil (a symbol of Holy Spirit) upon the head of the anointee.

His instruction involved preparing **Hazael for his crown** and **Jehu for his crown.** The act of anointing with oil occurred before the natural crown was placed upon Hazael's and Jehu's heads. But spiritually speaking...

In the case of Hazael and Jehu, the anointing prepared them for the crown.

1 Kings 19:16-18:

> ¹⁶ 'Also, you shall **anoint** Jehu the son of Nimshi as king over Israel. **And Elisha** the son of Shaphat of Abel Meholah, **you shall anoint as prophet in your place.**'

Elijah was to anoint his replacement.

Notice also that Elijah had a regional, multi-country jurisdiction—Syria and Israel.

The anointing is to destroy those who oppose God's purposes.

God designed a three-pronged defense.

> ¹⁷ 'It shall be that whoever escapes **the sword of Hazael, Jehu** will kill; and whoever escapes the sword of Jehu, **Elisha** will kill.
>
> ¹⁸ Yet I have reserved seven thousand in Israel, all whose knees have not bowed to Baal, and every mouth that has not kissed him.'

Another example of this is found in Exodus 29:4-7:

> ⁴ 'And Aaron and his sons you shall bring to the door of the tabernacle of meeting, and you shall wash them with water. ⁵ Then you shall take the garments, put the tunic on Aaron, and the robe of the ephod, the ephod, and the breastplate, and gird him with the intricately woven band of the ephod. ⁶ You shall put the turban on his head, and put **the holy crown** on the turban. ⁷ And

you shall take the anointing oil, pour it on his head, and anoint him. *(Emphasis mine)*

Wherever the LORD has placed you, you have specific blessings and anointings you are to capitalize on as sons.

The anointing empowers you to assert your authority!

Wear the crown and possess the land, for it is the gift of the LORD to you.

Zechariah 4:6:

> *So he answered and said to me: 'This is the word of the Lord to Zerubbabel: Not by might nor by power, but by My Spirit,' Says the Lord of hosts.*

Empowerment—which is a function of the anointing—comes not from human strength but from the Holy Spirit.

Psalm 89:20:

> *I have found My servant David; with My holy oil I have anointed him.*

Even though David was anointed physically, he experienced God's spiritual anointing over his kingship. This verse hints at the **sacredness** of that purpose.

The anointing serves a purpose, as we see in Luke 4:18-19:

> *^{18} The Spirit of the Lord is upon me, because he has **anointed me** to preach the Gospel to the poor; He has sent me to heal the brokenhearted, the proclaim liberty to the captives and recovery of sight to the blind, to set at liberty those who are oppressed. ^{19} To proclaim the acceptable year of the Lord. (Emphasis mine)*

Because Jesus had specific purposes, the Spirit of the Lord rested upon him. Because YOU have a particular purpose, the Spirit of the Lord rests upon *you*!

The anointing is in response to your purpose, not your lifestyle.

The anointing has nothing to do with your character, nor is it necessarily in response to your lifestyle. It is a response to your purpose. You can cooperate with the anointing upon your life by seeking after the Lord and living in obedience to the Father. Still, even unbelievers will experience an anointing to accomplish their purpose.

The anointing you experience can be released regardless of your lifestyle. The anointing is not condoning sin in your life, nor is it excusing sin in your life. The operation of the anointing through your life is also not an excuse to live an ungodly life. Live on purpose and *from* purpose.

I knew of a pastor who, although highly anointed in his ministry, was chasing as many skirts in the church as he could, and he was catching a few of them. Although his personal lifestyle was a train wreck, he was still anointed when he stood to preach. The anointing upon him was in response to his purpose, not his lifestyle. It will be the same with you. The anointing never condones your sin, nor does it excuse your sin. However, do yourself and everyone else a favor—live right! Don't leave a trail of trauma in your wake.

Hebrews 1:9 (Speaking of Jesus):

> *You have loved righteousness and hated lawlessness; therefore God, Your God, has anointed You with the oil of gladness more than Your companions.*

Living a life pursuing and fulfilling one's purposes will result in a more joyful existence. The anointing cannot be purchased with money, nor should it be stolen by stealth—the anointing results from the pressing of the grapes *and* the olives. If you have an anointing, guard it, shield yourself from vacuum cleaners, those who would seek to suck you dry, and finally, don't sell it or covet others anointings—honor them, but never covet them.

Romans 8:11:

But if the Spirit of Him who raised Jesus from the dead dwells in you, He who raised Christ from the dead will also give life to your mortal bodies through His Spirit who dwells in you.

Finally, the anointing is connected to resurrection life—divine empowerment lives inside the believer. Let's live from that strength and not our own.

———— ∞ ————

Chapter 10
Are You Wielding Your Scepter?

Scepters are, in a sense, ornamental staffs carried by rulers as a symbol of sovereignty. However, they are not merely ornamental. They are symbolic in Scripture of authority, kingship, righteous rule, and divine favor. As sons, we don't use scepters to fight our enemy, because a scepter is not a weapon. You don't wield a scepter to get to a place of authority...you wield a scepter because you are already IN a place of authority.

Scepters speak of authority, legitimacy, favor, and access, and righteousness and justice, which are the foundations of God's throne. Often, the word scepter was also translated as rod or staff. Each variation has a particular nuance: scepter—kingly authority and royal favor; rod—speaks of the power to enforce discipline, judgment, or firm rulership; and the staff speaks of tender guidance and leadership from a shepherding standpoint.

Psalm 23:4:

*Yea, though I walk through the valley of the shadow of death, I will fear no evil; for You are with me; Your **rod** and Your staff, they comfort me. (Emphasis mine)*

Angels are released to each of you for your places of assignment—they do the battling for you; they are equipped for it!

Psalm 45:6:

*Your throne, O God, is forever and ever; A **scepter of righteousness is the scepter of Your kingdom**. (Emphasis mine)*

Hebrews 1:8-9:

*⁸ But to the Son He says: 'Your throne, O God is forever and ever; **a scepter of righteousness is the scepter of your Kingdom**. ⁹ You have loved righteousness and hated lawlessness; therefore God, your God has anointed you with the oil of gladness more than your companions.' (Emphasis mine)*

> The Father is changing our mode of operation from "sword-based" to "scepter-based."

Psalm 125:3:

*For the **scepter of wickedness** shall not rest on the land allotted to the righteous, lest the righteous reach out their hands to iniquity. (Emphasis mine)*

Revelation 19:15-16:

*¹⁵ Now out of <u>His mouth</u> goes a sharp sword, that with it He should strike the nations. And He Himself will rule them with **a rod (scepter) of iron**. He Himself treads the winepress of the fierceness and wrath of Almighty God.*

¹⁶ And He has on His robe and on His thigh a name written: King of kings and Lord of lords. (Emphasis mine)

Psalms 2:8-9

*⁸ Ask of Me, and **I will give you the nations for your inheritance,** and the ends of the Earth for your possession.*

*⁹ You shall break them with **a rod (scepter) of iron**; you shall dash them to pieces like a potter's vessel. (Emphasis mine)*

How do you wield a Scepter?

It is a staff—some are about 6-7 feet tall (usually ornamental on the top). Some are much shorter. In the spirit, hold it in your right hand (the hand of strength). You can be seated or standing, then extend your scepter out from your body, point in the direction of the situation needing governance, and declare the will of Heaven over the situation. From your position—you rule! Never rule from assumption—*only from position!*

Remember...

- You are *in* authority because you are *under* authority.
- You are to rule *in* and *from* your places of assignment, not battle from them.
- If you were not qualified, you would not have received the scepter.
- You can either further qualify yourself or disqualify yourself based on how you handle the responsibility given.
- Rule with righteousness. Let that be your first motivation—to establish righteousness where you are!
- Finally...

Rule by scepter, not by sword!

We must:

1. **Recognize that you have received your scepter.** (See Luke 10:19 and Romans 5:17). Know that the Father has already extended royal favor to you because you are His son.
2. **Stand in His righteousness.** It is called the "scepter of righteousness" in Hebrews 1:8. To

wield it, your character needs to align with his righteousness. Authority flows through purity and right standing with God.

3. **Speak with authority.** Kings rule by decrees because the authority of their office backs their word. Wielding your scepter often involves declaring God's Word over situations and circumstances. You aren't pleading, you are declaring *from a position of strength*. As an ambassador, you are releasing the will of the King into situations. You wield your scepter when you *speak in faith, align with Heaven,* and *have confidence in your position.* Angels will then do their part in fulfilling your declaration. *Angels know when you are confident in what you say. Never speak* from a position of hope. Speak from a place of *confident knowing*.

4. **Extend mercy and justice.** You extend the Father's heart to those you wield the scepter toward. Sometimes you will rebuke darkness, and at other times welcome the broken. Righteous authority is not cold power; it is *compassion married to strength*.

5. **Stay yielded to the King.** The Father is the source of any authority you carry. True wielding happens when you continually *listen, obey,* and *yield* to the King of kings. It is not about ruling for your will to be done. It is establishing His Kingdom on Earth as it already is in Heaven.

Now, request access to the Court of Crowns and let's request the following:

Court Scenario

Father, I request access to the Court of Crowns. For every crown I have received, I request the full release of the scepters accompanying these crowns.

I declare:

*I will **stand** in righteousness, clothed in the Anointed One—Jesus Christ.*

*I will **speak** Your Word with authority and love.*

*I will **extend** mercy, justice, and truth wherever You send me.*

*I will **govern** my life, my family, and my sphere with Heaven's wisdom.*

*I will **yield** continually to Your Spirit, never trusting in my own strength.*

By Your Spirit, teach me:

- *when to decree,*
- *when to extend favor,*
- *when to rebuke darkness, and*
- *when to shepherd with tenderness.*

I arise today under the covering of the King. I embrace the call to rule with Christ—in purity, in power, and in perfect surrender.

Let my life be a reflection of Your righteous reign, and may Your Kingdom come and Your will be done on Earth as it is in Heaven—through me.

Thank you, Father.

Daily Declaration: Wielding My Scepter

Father, today, I arise in my authority as a son.

I receive Your scepter of righteousness and favor.

I rule my life, my home, and my calling with Your wisdom and strength.

I speak life, decree truth, and extend mercy.

As a son, I break every assignment of darkness by the power of Jesus' name.

I am led by Your Spirit, clothed in Your righteousness, and empowered by Your grace.

Today, I rule and reign with Christ—for Your glory and the advancement of Your Kingdom.

I will not shrink back.

I am crowned, anointed, and commissioned.

The King's authority rests upon me.

I will reign in life through Jesus, my elder brother, today!

———— ∞ ————

Chapter 11
Are You Demonstrating The Glory?

Another typical package of a crown involves the Glory of God that you carry because of the crown you possess.

Each crown has a specific release of the Glory associated with it.

We don't often think of ourselves as carriers of the Glory, but Heaven sees us that way.

The Glory is the expression of Heaven into the Earth realm.

The Word of God says that if Christ is in us, so is the Glory (Colossians 1:27).

Colossians 1:26-29

*²⁶ There is a divine mystery—a secret surprise that has been concealed from the world for generations, but now it's being revealed, unfolded, and manifested **for every holy believer to experience.** ²⁷ **Living within you is the Christ who floods you with the expectation of glory!** This mystery¹³ of **Christ, embedded within us,** becomes a heavenly treasure chest of hope filled with **the riches of glory for his people,** and God wants everyone to know it!*

*²⁸⁻²⁹ Christ is our message! We preach to awaken hearts and bring every person into the full understanding of truth. It has become my inspiration and passion in ministry to labor with a tireless intensity, with **his power flowing through me, to present to every believer the revelation of being his perfect one in Jesus Christ.** (TPT)*

Paul wrote in Ephesians 1:16-23:

¹⁶ ...I do not cease to give thanks for you, making mention of you in my prayers: ¹⁷ that the God of

---

[13] Part of the mystery is that this is an expression of quantum mechanics, specifically the Law of Quantum Entanglement which is a fairly recent scientific understanding. In Paul's day, they did not have language for it, but now we do.

our Lord Jesus Christ, **the Father of glory,** *may give to you the spirit of wisdom and revelation in the knowledge of Him,* [18] *the eyes of your understanding being enlightened; that you may know what is the hope of His calling, what are* **the riches of the glory of His inheritance in the saints,** [19] *and what is the exceeding greatness of His power toward us who believe, according to the working of His mighty power* [20] *which He worked in Christ when He raised Him from the dead and seated Him at His right hand in the heavenly places,* [21] *far above all principality and power and might and dominion, and every name that is named, not only in this age but also in that which is to come.* [22] *And He put all things under His feet, and gave Him to be head over all things to the church,* [23] *which is His body, the fullness of Him who fills all in all.* (Emphasis mine)

The Glory of the Lord is an entity as well as an expression. In Ezekiel 10:18:

Then the glory of the LORD departed from the threshold of the temple and **stood** *over the cherubim.*

The Glory of the Lord can stand. As we walk in the authority of the crowns of Heaven—expressing the mantle, seated on the throne of that crown, exercising the dominion granted to us, and operating in the anointing of that crown—the Glory of God will manifest through our lives. As we wield the scepter we have been given, we will begin to walk in a level of strength we have not known. We will *speak into* **and** *govern situations* by what we carry because we know WHO we are and WHOSE we are!

I John 4:4:

> *Greater is he that is in you than he that is in the world.*

As you are living from your crown, release the Glory into the dominion of that crown. Allow the Glory to permeate every aspect of that dominion. Release the Glory to the north, south, east, and west, as well as above and below, and in every age, realm, and dimension.

The Glory changes things!

The Glory is the invasion of Heaven into the Earth realm.

Five Things the Glory Provides

1. Identity and Sonship

The Glory of God confirms who you are. When you're in His presence, confusion about your worth or calling melts away. You're not just tolerated—you're celebrated. His Glory seals your identity as a beloved son or daughter of the King.

2. Rest and Peace

Where His Glory dwells, striving ends. You stop trying to earn love or force outcomes. Instead, you step into divine rest, trusting that God's presence is more than enough to carry you, provide for you, and fight for you.

3. Transformation and Healing

God's Glory is not just bright—it's purifying. *In His presence, deep wounds get healed, chains fall off, and old mindsets are renewed*—not just from you, but those you impact with your life. What used to feel impossible begins to shift effortlessly.

4. Revelation and Clarity

The Glory brings light—supernatural understanding of His ways and His will. Things that were foggy become clear. You begin to see from Heaven's perspective and walk in divine wisdom.

5. Empowerment and Authority

His Glory clothes you with power. It's not just about feeling His nearness, it's about being equipped to represent Him. The Glory empowers you to walk in spiritual authority, make bold decisions, and carry Heaven into every sphere you touch.

Bryan and Katie Torwalt wrote a song entitled "When You Walk into the Room,"[14] describing the impact of Jesus when He enters our situations. However, we often miss an important truth that Jesus wants us to understand: When we, as believers, walk into a room, He enters with us. The lyrics of the first verse say:

> *When You walk into the room, everything changes*
>
> *Darkness starts to tremble at the light that You bring*
>
> *And when You walk into the room, every heart starts burning*
>
> *And nothing matters more than just to sit here at Your feet and worship You*
>
> *We worship You*

---

[14] © 2013 Jesus Culture (Admin. by Jesus Culture Music).

This song expresses the truth that when Jesus walks into a situation, everything can change. Let's realize that when *we* walk into a room, Jesus walks in too.

*When **you** walk into the room, everything changes*

*Darkness starts to tremble at the light that **you** bring*

We can be the ones walking into a room, affecting change. If we, by intention, release the Glory wherever we go, we will begin to see changes in the atmosphere wherever we are. Where turmoil may have been reigning, peace now reigns. Where sickness may have been dominant, its effect is lessening. Religion has taught us to be so self-effacing that we disregard the fact that it is in us that Jesus lives, moves, and has His being now.

In Isaiah 60:1, Isaiah wrote:

Arise, shine; For your light has come! And the glory of the LORD is risen upon you.

Some translations render it, "Arise, shine. Be light."

When we walk into a room, everything should shift—atmospheres, attitudes, actions—because we are carriers of a superior source of life, the Glory of God.

Habakkuk 2:14:

For the earth will be filled with the knowledge of **the glory of the LORD**, *as the waters cover the sea. (Emphasis mine)*

The word knowledge comes from the Hebrew *yada* and implies an intimate knowledge instead of a mental ascent to a concept. *Yada* is the word used in Genesis 4:1:

Now Adam **knew** *(yada) Eve his wife, and she conceived and bore Cain, and said, 'I have acquired a man from the LORD.' (Emphasis mine)*

It took more than a mental ascent for Cain to be conceived. An intimate knowledge of Eve occurred as he became one with her, and the result was the conception of Cain.

If the Earth is filled with an intimate knowledge of the Glory, believers may be required to become intimate with the Father. The people of the Earth and the Earth itself will have an intimate encounter with the Glory of the Lord. That intimacy will cover the Earth as the waters cover the sea.

Once we understand who we are and what has been deposited in us, we can walk into Walmart and change the atmosphere. Wherever you go, step into the strength of the crowns you possess, and as you walk down the aisle of the frozen foods section, release the Glory. As you go down the cereal aisle, release the Glory. Wherever you go, release the Glory.

The Glory will settle the chaos, which is often part of the store's atmosphere. It will help settle the small children who had been agitated only moments before. It will effect change! The effect will be transformation!

The Glory changes atmospheres!

Many can quote 1 John 4:4, but do we truly believe it?

You are of God, little children, and **have overcome** *them,* <u>because</u> **He who is in you is greater than he who is in the world.** *(Emphasis mine)*

How do I know? Look at your life and ask yourself, "Am I more a victim than a victor?"

Do things happen to me,
or do things happen
because I effect change?

If you are the victim more than the victor, this verse and its truth are not yet real to you, but they can be. You must settle within yourself that God has already proven his love to you. He needs not do another thing to prove to you that He loves you.

John 3:16:

> *For God **so loved** the world that He gave His only begotten Son, that whoever believes in Him should not perish but have everlasting life.*

The enemy likes to challenge people with, "If God loved you, why did He let this happen? No! Settle it in your soul. He already proved his love on the cross. Love has been proven! Then, when things happen *to* you, you are not moved by them. The Father's love for you is settled.

The events that occur in my life are not accidental. They are orchestrated. I live out of purpose, *and* I live <u>on purpose</u>! It is a vastly different way of living that many have yet to experience. I understand that because I have a purpose, I can live out of that purpose, and things happen *for* me, not *to* me. Nothing in my life is by accident.

Psalms 37:23:

> *The steps of a good man are ordered by the LORD, and He delights in his way.*

Ordered can also be translated as to set up, establish, fix, prepared, appointed, rendered, or made prosperous: confirmed, directed, fashioned, ordained, have made provision for.

In Proverbs 16:9, we read:

> *Within your heart you can make plans for your future, but the Lord chooses the steps you take to get there. (TPT)*

God is setting you up for your future—a future to be lived out of sonship, not out of happenstance. I choose to live out of purpose. **You can also live out of purpose!** I recommend it! This is made even more real because I have received the crowns associated with this purpose. You will want to do the same.

Begin living out of your purpose upon the Earth!

Once we believe the words of 1 John 4:4, things will change around us. As we walk in this understanding, we will see ourselves walking intentionally. We will see our part in releasing the Glory in the Earth, and we will fulfill our responsibility before the Lord. **Nothing happens that is not permitted.**

The words of Jesus will take on new meaning as we understand our responsibility, see Matthew 6:33-34:

> *33 'So above all, **constantly chase after the realm of God's kingdom** and the righteousness that proceeds from him. Then, all these less important things will be given to you abundantly. 34 Refuse to worry about tomorrow, but deal with each challenge that comes your way, one day at a time. Tomorrow will take care of itself.' (TPT) (Emphasis mine)*

> *Refuse to be distracted by distractions.*

The enemy would like for you to constantly be concerned about paying your bills, stomping out little fires in your life, and not having the bandwidth left to extend the Kingdom of Heaven on the Earth. These are less important things. They are distractions for sons. Don't take the bait!

Being Heavenly Minded

Many have heard the phrase, "He is so heavenly minded, he is no earthly good." However, we need to revisit that saying. One day, the Holy Spirit spoke to me about that saying and said, "That was spoken out of a mocking spirit." My friend Heidi has an entirely different take on that saying:

> *I want to be so heavenly-minded that I am earthly incredible!*

In Colossians, Paul instructs us in Colossians 3:1-3:

> *¹ If then you were raised with Christ, **seek those things which are above**, where Christ is, sitting at the right hand of God. ² **Set your mind on things above, not on things on the earth.***

> *³ For you died, and your life is hidden with Christ in God. (Emphasis mine)*

The Passion Translation translates the passage this way:

> *¹ Christ's resurrection is **your** resurrection too. This is why **we are to yearn for all that is above**, for that's where Christ sits enthroned at the place of all power, honor, and authority! ² Yes, feast on all the treasures of the heavenly realm and **fill your thoughts with heavenly realities, and not with the distractions of the natural realm.** ³ Your crucifixion with Christ has severed the tie to this life, and **now your true life is hidden away in God in Christ.** (Colossians 3:1-3) (TPT) (Emphasis mine)*

Rather than giving heed to the mocking of that old phrase used to discredit those who were more conscious of Heaven than of Earth. We should seek to emulate those saints and introduce Heaven into the Earth with them. We are instructed to set our minds on Heaven and the realms of Heaven. To be so conscious of the earthly realm is to be in direct disobedience to the instruction of Colossians 3:1.

Once you become aware of this, the entire New Testament reiterates the concept. It was not merely a transitory suggestion.

The Gospel of Matthew was written to introduce us to the realm of Heaven's Kingdom and how it applies to our lives on Earth. As we live out of this realm, living the truths of Jesus' Sermon on the Mount becomes easy. We will find ourselves living the beatitudes. The instructions of Jesus will not be complicated. They will be the natural outgrowth of a relationship centered on Heaven and introducing Heaven to the world around you. Fruit grows on plants because it is connected to the root system. As we are rooted and grounded in Jesus, producing fruit that reflects him will naturally occur. We will not have to attempt to make it happen! It is a superior way of living.

I am not speaking of living in a manner that makes you seem "zoned out" from the world around you. On the contrary, you may be quite cognizant of the world around you, but even more, you will be cognizant of the world surrounding *that* world—the *real* world. We must realize that Heaven is the real, and this Earth realm is the vapor.[15] Where we reside now will pass away, but the realm of Heaven is eternal.

According to Romans 9:23-24, we have been chosen to experience the Glory:

> *²³ And doesn't he also have the right to release the revelation of the wealth of his glory to his*

---

[15] James 4:14, Psalm 39:5, Psalm 39:11, Psalm 62:9, 2 Corinthians 4:18

vessels of mercy, **whom God prepared beforehand to receive his glory?** *²⁴ Even for us, whether we are Jews or non-Jews, we are those* **he has called to experience his glory.** *(TPT)*

God decided long ago that we should be partakers of His Glory, but not *just* partakers, but to experience His Glory.

I Corinthians 2:7:

It is his secret plan, destined before the ages, to bring us into glory. (TPT)

This is not a last-minute decision! It has been God's plan all along! We GET to participate! Let God show up in that dominion and let the Glory permeate our surroundings. Let Him show up *in you!*

Father, I embrace the Glory that is part of this crown. I choose to walk in agreement with Heaven and allow the release of the Glory as I walk in the strength of this crown You have granted me. Thank You.

———— ∞ ————

Chapter 12
Are You Accessing the Resources?

In order to facilitate the anointing, dominion, and other aspects of a crown, certain resources—property, finances, personnel, and more—are allocated by Heaven. Without these resources being released to the sons, we will be hindered in fulfilling our scroll and the intent of the crown.

Earlier, we spoke of capacity—the space that crowns provide and possess. Each crown carries a specific capacity, and that capacity is contained in Him.

When it comes to intercession, you will have a specific capacity based on your scroll—the written intent of the Father for you. One way to enlarge your capacity is through a paradoxical act: cast your crowns into the capacity of this space, and when they return, they will have expanded. Casting your crowns is not taking them away from you. It's adding to you. Just try it."

Instructions: *Now, you, the reader, pause and cast the Crown of Revelation Receiver you obtained at the beginning of this book. Cast it into this space called capacity. It will come back to you.*

Stephanie replied, "Okay, so I cast my Crown of Endurance into the capacity of this space. When I did, I saw the crown illuminate."

Lydia asked, "Is your crown *not* your authority?"

"Yes."

Your crown is your authority.

"Then use your authority to call in the treasure."

---
*Use your authority
to call in the treasure (the resources).*

Stephanie immediately responded:

As a son, I call in the treasures and resources that have been lost or stolen from the north, the south, the east, and the west in every age, realm, dimension, and time to fill the capacity of this section.

She noted, "I saw, as I threw it out, it was just a section of the capacity. I see from this Crown of

Endurance that waterfalls begin to form. It's as if we are creating in this capacity in this place, which is like a blank slate to fill.

"We would claim the land, properties, houses, and commercial properties that have been lost. We call them back to us. We claim that here as we cast that crown."

Stephanie replied:

In my authority, I cast all my crowns into the space that encompasses the north, south, east, and west. As a governing son, I make a proclamation and a statement: All stolen from me will return to me, beginning now.

With my Crown of Authority, I stand and govern because of Jesus. I make a demand in the spirit for those things lost, stolen, or forfeited to be brought back sevenfold,[16] to fill the capacity given to me to hold and entrusted to me as a son in the name of Jesus. May every room be filled, every indention, every depth, and every height.[17]

Lydia reminded us of 1 Corinthians 2:9-10:

[9] But as it is written: 'Eye has not seen, nor ear heard, nor have entered into the heart of man the things which God has prepared for those who love him.' [10] But God has revealed them to

---

[16] Proverbs 6:31
[17] See Ephesians 3:14-21

us through His Spirit. For the Spirit searches all things, yes, the deep things of God.

This is life
and that more abundantly.

We then found ourselves in a courtroom, and Stephanie began:

Lord, I present to You the books of my generations—the books of all the prayers and supplications that have gone forth, and now the crowns that have been reestablished. I also present the capacity You are showing us to present to You.

I call forth the restoration of my generations. In every place we have had crowns and resources, territories, inheritances, finances, children, peace, houses, vineyards, gifts, and callings lost, stolen, or forfeited, I ask that they be re-established. I ask that they be put on record and placed in our books to fill the capacity to the brim more than we could think or imagine. I request a release from the North, South, East, and West.

I commission the angels to go to those reservoirs, those hiding places where things were stolen and taken, and to bring them back in their fullness. As a governing son, I take the riches of Heaven, the riches in the earth that have been given to us.

I am thankful for this court, the knowledge and understanding, and the capacity You have given me. May God be glorified.

Lydia began to instruct us:

1. **The first step is to visit the Court of Crowns and obtain renewed authorization for the authority that has been lost.** Request that of the court, having done repentance for losing that crown.
2. **Then, commission the angels to begin bringing in what has been lost and fill the capacity.** That capacity can also be enlarged.

Stephanie prayed:

Where I laid down my authority, or my generations did, and stepped out of my jurisdiction, I want to acknowledge that and take responsibility for it. I repent of it and ask that the authority and territory taken be restored and reestablished in the name of Jesus.

I ask this court for a renewed authorization of the authority lost due to the forfeiture of my crown(s).

I also thank the court for the establishment and the capacity of the promised land that has not been able to come forth because of my not governing correctly as a son. Still, I now understand the capacity of what I am and whose I am as I take in the territory, the lands, the inheritances, and all that has been established here in the name of Jesus.

I commission the angels to bring these things from this place into the natural realm on behalf of the sons so that I may be a good steward of what You have given me.

As Stephanie prayed, she got a bird's eye view of the Court of Crowns and realized we were inside a crown.

You want your angels' involvement in restoring the lost, stolen, or forfeited resources so the process can begin. Many of us may have just now started to have some resources restored. It is standing in your sonship and commissioning angels to bring what has been stolen into your hands. As you walk out more and more of your sonship and sonship rights, you will benefit from angels co-laboring and men and women in white assisting and counseling you along the way. Entities of Heaven, such as Lady Wisdom, will also come alongside to help, especially when you invite them to co-labor with you.

As sons, we should not be in a deficit in any area. When Peter wrote that God has given us ALL THINGS[18] that pertain to life and godliness, he meant ALL THINGS. Everything you need to fulfill your scroll upon

---

[18] 2 Peter 1:3

the Earth and in the Heavens has been placed at your disposal.

Begin to govern resources.

Demand their appearance in your realm and watch the words that come out of your mouth to ensure they align with what your spirit knows to be the case.

Now that you understand more about what a crown entails, you can begin to make progress in fulfilling your scroll. It is hard to fulfill it when you don't know everything involved. You now know that every crown has a mantle, a throne, a dominion, an anointing, a scepter, Glory, and specific resources. With this knowledge, you can begin to place a demand in the spirit for those things to perform their work in the realms to which they are assigned.

———— ∞ ————

Chapter 13

The Crown of Life

As we engaged Heaven, we could see, in the Library of Revelation, bookcases on one side of the table, and on the table was a crown. It was placed on a beautiful red fabric. Jesus was standing to one side with Mary, his mother. She took the crown and began wrapping the red cloth around it. We could see the tender care with which she wrapped it and could sense that she knew that the storage of this crown was only temporary. The crucifixion wasn't the end of Jesus. She wrapped it and handed it to Joseph of Arimathea.

As she handed the crown to him, the room changed, and Stephanie could see them place the crown wrapped in cloth in the tomb. Both leaned over and kissed the fabric containing the crown. They walked out, and the stone was rolled over the entrance.

Again, the scene changed. Now she was back in the library, and Jesus had stepped forward from her left and sat at the head of the table. He asked her, "What crown do you think that is?"

Jesus answered His question by saying, "It's the Crown of Life."

He took her back to the inside of the tomb, and she could see the crown begin to illuminate beneath the fabric. It began lighting the room.

Jesus said, "The moment the stone closed the entry, this crown became illuminated." As he spoke, she saw His body rise. He stood, placed the crown on His head, and walked down a stairway into hell. He was barefoot, wearing only His tunic.

Smoke rose from the pit, and the stairway disappeared into utter darkness. Jesus invited her to walk with Him. She joined Him, and together they descended the steps into the depths.

Stephanie said, "Jesus, I felt like when You arose and put on this crown, and this place—hell—opened up. I feel like You willingly walked down there, just like You willingly died."

He said, "I did."

Stephanie could not see past Jesus as he walked down the steps into the darkness. She waited on the stairway for Him to return. She saw Him return, and he was bringing many crowns with him.

He said, "The moment I took the keys of death, hell, and the grave is the same moment I took the Crowns of Life for the sons."

Stephanie could see all these people coming behind Him. As they walked up the steps, Jesus turned and began handing crowns to those coming out of the darkness with Him. As they received their Crown of Life, they placed it on their heads.

Revelation 2:10:

Do not yield to fear in the face of the suffering to come, but be aware of this: the devil is about to have some of you thrown into prison to test your faith. For ten days you will have distress, but remain faithful to the day you die and I will give you the victor's **crown of life**. *(TPT) (Emphasis mine)*

James 1:12:

If your faith remains strong, even while surrounded by life's difficulties, you will continue to experience the untold blessings of God! True happiness comes as you pass the test with faith and receive the victorious **crown of life** *promised to every lover of God! (TPT) (Emphasis mine)*

Jesus approached Stephanie, placed a crown on her head, kissed her cheek, and smiled.

As she watched the scene, she saw that they continued walking up a stairway into Heaven as they received their crown. Jesus said, "We walked up these stairs after we had a little fun in the streets."

She asked, "Are you talking about where people saw the dead had risen?"

He said, "This *IS* the Crown of Life. I died to give life and that more abundantly."

The scene changed once more, and they were back at the table. Jesus said, "Many sons have rejected the Crown of Life. I went into Sheol to display life."

She noticed that he was showing her a wedding band and was holding her hand. He said, "This is a bought and paid for price. Every son has this crown, but some reject Jesus."

Stephanie asked, "Can we enter the Court of Crowns for those we know who are not yet saved and request this for them? I know You have already secured it, but as sons who wear this crown, are we able to intercede—not asking for something new, but for what has already been given?"

He explained that we can **request the illumination of this crown upon their heads because they are His.** We asked Him to show us what to do.

He instructed us to go into the Court of Crowns, and He just said to ask. Ask the Father, the Just Judge.

Stephanie stepped into the Court of Crowns and petitioned the Just Judge:

I ask for the crowns upon the heads of those I love who rejected Jesus to be illuminated because of Jesus, because of the wedding band—the promise—because he went into utter darkness for them, so that they are given a chance because they belong to Jesus.

On behalf of my family members who rejected You, I want to say, 'I am so sorry. I repent on their behalf and on behalf of the many in my generations who rejected Your crown, even though it was still on their heads.'

But You love them. Thank You for entering into utter darkness and choosing it, yet wearing this crown—the Crown of Life.

I ask that their crowns be illuminated with life and that life more abundantly. When people see us, they see this crown.

Stephanie then saw a piece of paper in his hand, and she could see the names of those she loved who rejected the crown. Their names lit up. It was as if it was just written in black ink, and now she could see them illuminating.

Jesus said, "I did this for the sons, but think of this as a co-laboring. I use my sons on behalf of <u>all</u> the sons. What I did was once and for all. And because of my love for you, I use each of you in the process."

He then showed her the Court of Supplications[19] and that when we look through this book for people we are praying for, we can look at the crowns, whether they are illuminated or not, just like we could see if our prayer was not rejected. If we needed to determine the legal right, we could see if this crown was illuminated. Thank you, Jesus, for this Crown of Life.

The Promise of the Crown of Life

James 1:12:

> *If your faith remains strong, even while surrounded by life's difficulties, you will continue to experience the untold blessings of God! True happiness comes as you pass the test with faith, and receive* ***the victorious crown of life promised to every lover of God!*** *(TPT) (Emphasis mine)*

Revelation 2:10:

> *Do not yield to fear in the face of the suffering to come, but be aware of this: the devil is about to have some of you thrown into prison to test your faith. For ten days you will have distress, but remain faithful to the day you die and I will give*

---

[19] *Next Dimension Access to the Court of Supplications* by Dr. Ron M. Horner, LifeSpring Publishing (2024).

> *you **the victor's crown of life**. (TPT) (Emphasis mine)*

As we pondered these verses, he showed Stephanie an image of someone on their deathbed that never served Jesus, and that as they call out to Him at their death, He places a Crown of Life on them. Jesus said, "I've come that they may have life, and they may have it more abundantly."[20]

That would explain why when we come and intercede on behalf of our loved ones, we can ask for the illumination of that crown upon their heads just as things such as air, food, and water are vital for our physical lives. Jesus provides us with what is required for our spiritual lives. He is the one who provides living water. He's the Bread of Life—eternal life, and this is the promise that He has made to us.

This answered a question she had. She had wondered how they could receive a Crown of Life when they had not suffered according to the verse in Revelation.

Jesus explained, "This Crown of Life is for all who love God. Even those people that did not serve God in their life, but on their deathbed cry out to Jesus who will give them the Crown of Life."

---

[20] John 10:10

He said, "How much do you think they suffered to that point?"

Stephanie admitted, "I don't know."

He replied, "They suffered a lifetime without God."

They experience utter loneliness and hopelessness.

This parable explains it well. Matthew 20:1-16:

> *¹ This will help you understand the way heaven's kingdom operates: 'There once was a wealthy landowner who went out at daybreak to hire all the laborers he could find to work in his vineyard. ² After agreeing to pay them the standard day's wage, he put them to work. ³ Then at nine o'clock, as he was passing through the town square, he found others standing around without work. ⁴ He told them, 'Come and work for me in my vineyard and I'll pay you a fair wage.' ⁵ So off they went to join the others. He did the same thing at noon and again at three o'clock, making the same arrangement as he did with the others.*
>
> *⁶ Hoping to finish his harvest that day, he went to the town square again at five o'clock and found more who were idle. So he said to them, 'Why have you been here all day without work?'*
>
> *⁷ 'Because no one hired us,' they answered. So he said to them, 'Then go and join my crew and work in my vineyard.'*

8 When evening came, the owner of the vineyard went to his foreman and said, 'Call in all the laborers, line them up, and pay them the same wages, starting with the most recent ones I hired and finishing with the ones who worked all day.' 9 When those hired late in the day came to be paid, they were given a full day's wage. 10 And when those who had been hired first came to be paid, they were convinced that they would receive more. But everyone was paid the standard wage.

11 When they realized what had happened, they were offended and complained to the landowner, saying, 12 'You're treating us unfairly! They've only worked for one hour while we've slaved and sweated all day under the scorching sun. You've made them equal to us!'

13 'The landowner replied, 'Friends, I'm not being unfair—I'm doing exactly what I said. Didn't you agree to work for the standard wage? 14 If I want to give those who only worked for an hour equal pay, what does that matter to you?

15 *'Don't I have the right to do what I want with what is mine? Why should my generosity make you jealous of them?'*

16 'Now you can understand what I meant when I said that the first will end up last and the last will end up being first. Everyone is invited, but few are the chosen.' (TPT) (Emphasis mine)

Just as the laborers hired in the late afternoon received the same wages as those who had labored all day, it's up to the vineyard owner how generous he wants to be.

Jesus said, "What if I told you that I rescued the one who cried out for a bit of water for his tongue?" He said, "I want that none should perish."

Unlike what religion does, Jesus is making it easy to get into Heaven. Many have been taught that if we do one thing wrong, we are going to hell. That belief system keeps us in a state of insecurity about our salvation. The Father is far more merciful than most preachers.

Stephanie prayed:

Father, thank You for rescuing that man. Thank You for the Crown of Life that You give everyone and for having the final say in hell and Sheol.

———— ∞ ————

Chapter 14

The Crown of the Lamb

As we began this engagement with Heaven, Stephanie heard the lyrics to the old hymn, "It is Well with My Soul." Specifically, she heard the lines that said, "When peace like a river attendeth my way, when sorrows like sea billows roll...."[21]

Someone from Heaven spoke, "What if sorrow can be changed in an instant?"

"That would be awesome," we replied.

They remarked, "If sorrow comes as sea billow's roll, that would seem to overwhelm and overcome you. Jesus took sorrow on the cross. He *became* sorrow."

Stephanie saw a storm building on an ocean with the waves becoming stronger by the moment. Jesus

---

[21] Horatio Gates Spafford (1828-1888)

appeared, wearing a crown, and interrupted the vision by taking her to the tomb scene she had seen in a prior recent engagement, where he walked down a set of stairs into hell.

Jesus said, "I went into the depths of sorrow. I came up as *Conquering King*. I conquered the sorrows. It's no accident that you're seeing a storm in the natural." He *became* sorrow!

Stephanie was amid a storm that was passing through where she lived. She was having a visual representation of how sorrow comes, precisely like that storm. It arrived quickly and passed over quickly. The danger that you feel, the uncertainty, and the crashing thunderous sounds that come in sorrow. She watched as Jesus walked back up the stairs.

Jesus said, "I conquered that." Speaking of the overwhelming storm of sorrow.

Stephanie remarked, "I don't think I've ever thought of it, Jesus, that when you conquered everything, that sorrow was included. It doesn't say we'll have sorrows. It says trials. We will have trials on this Earth, but I'm realizing, Jesus, that you took on our sorrows. I've never heard it preached about specifically. I've heard it preached that you conquered disease—by your stripes, we are healed."

Jesus replied, "You are healed, but emotionally *and* mentally too."

Stephanie continued, "Jesus, when we have someone we love very much die, there is sorrow."

Jesus corrected her, saying, "There is grief."

Stephanie continued, "Okay, help me with this, Jesus, because I've thought many times that I have been sorrowful because I did X, Y and Z."

Jesus explained, "Sorrow is an entity. It's a spirit, and I've conquered it."

Stephanie noted, "As soon as he said, 'I conquered it,' it started pouring rain in the natural here. It hasn't rained until now."

Jesus said, "Sorrow overwhelms. Does that sound like the Kingdom of Heaven?"

Stephanie answered, "No."

We have been translated into the Library of Revelation, where a crown is on the table. The scripture he has given me is, "Lift up your heads, O you Gates, that the King of Glory may come in."[22]

She continued, "Jesus. I see the crown on the table on top of this book." Looking up, she saw Jesus weeping with tears streaming down his face.

Jesus said, "I took on your sorrows, so you didn't have to. You don't have to be overwhelmed by it. You

---

[22] Psalm 24:9

don't have to carry it. I went into the *depths of sorrows and* came out of it the *Conquering King.*"

Stephanie replied, "I have heard this a second time and now a third time, 'Lift up your heads, O ye gates, for the King of Glory is coming in.'"

Jesus came from one side of the table, I came from around the other side, and we are standing together. We both have our hands touching a piece of this crown. I can feel it. The scripture came to mind, "He will wipe away every tear, there'll be no more sorrow."

I had written a scripture in the chat for Stephanie to read from Isaiah 53:3-5:

> *³ He is despised and rejected by men, a Man of sorrows and acquainted with grief. and we hid, as it were, our faces from Him; He was despised, and we did not esteem Him.*
>
> *⁴ Surely He has borne our griefs and* **carried our sorrows***; yet we esteemed Him stricken, Smitten by God, and afflicted. ⁵ But He was wounded for our transgressions, He was bruised for our iniquities; the chastisement for our peace was upon Him, and by His stripes we are healed. (Emphasis mine)*

---

*He carried our sorrows
so we would not have to.*

Stephanie remarked, "As I watched him walk down the stairs into the pit of hell where he said he went into the depths of sorrows, the scripture *He will wipe away every tear, and they have no more sorrow* came to mind."

Three scriptures speak of this.

Isaiah 25:8:

*Swallow up death forever and **the Lord of God will wipe away tears from all faces**. (Emphasis mine)*

Revelation 7:17:

*...for the Lamb who is in the midst of the throne will shepherd them and lead them to living fountains of waters. And **God will wipe away every tear from their eyes**. (Emphasis mine)*

Revelation 21:4:

*And **God will wipe away every tear from their eyes**. There'll be no more death or sorrow nor mourning. There shall be no more pain for the former things have passed away. (Emphasis mine)*

Revelation 21:4-5:

***He wipes every tear from their eyes** and **blots out every hurtful memory**. And death shall be no more. Nor any association with it; no more mourning and bitter weeping nor any*

> *reference to pain. For the former things have passed away. (MIRROR) (Emphasis mine)*
>
> *⁵ And the one seated upon the throne said, 'Behold, **I make all things new.**'*

(That's the same thing as the amendment of "As If It Never Were.")

> *⁶ Anyone thirsty can come and drink freely from the gift of the waters of life direct from its source. ⁷ The **conquering one inherits all things,** and I will be God to him, and he will be my son. (Emphasis mine)*

Stephanie asked, "Jesus, what is this crown? Is this the Crown of Conquering, or the Conquering King, because it would be upon your head?"

Jesus replied, "This is the Crown of the Lamb."

Stephanie was then prompted to share an experience from the prior Sunday:

> *Yesterday, during praise and worship, I was taken to the feet of the cross where Jesus died, and I sang to Him. I realized that many other people were singing there as well. Towards the song's end, it says, 'You are high and lifted up,' and 'Worthy is the Lamb.' Suddenly, Jesus wasn't there on the cross anymore. I mean, I had come to his feet and had a hold of his feet.*

At one point, I was singing and praising in spirit and truth. Suddenly, I realized He wasn't there anymore, and there was just a hole in the ground where the cross had once been. I began singing to the Earth, 'We bless the Earth where this happened, to open up the victory, the victory that IS there.'

On the day of Jesus' crucifixion, He wore this crown. Just as they used to sacrifice lambs, Jesus was the ultimate sacrifice that day. Jesus wore the Crown of the Lamb. He took it upon himself.

In the engagement, Jesus picked up the Crown of the Lamb and held it in front of her, saying, 'No more sorrows means no more sorrows.'

Then, He put it on His head. As she looked down at the table, another crown was on it.

Jesus said, 'Pick it up.'

Stephanie picked it up and held it in front of herself.

Jesus asked Stephanie, 'Did you not die with me, and are you not raised with me?'

'Yes, Jesus, but I don't pretend to understand that.'

Jesus said, 'If you're in Me and I'm in you, you died with Me. I was wearing the Crown of the Lamb. No more sorrows. Put it on.'

Stephanie began to put it on, and Jesus said, 'Don't do it reluctantly. Put it on! Do you put on Christ? Is that not what the Word says?'

'Yes.'

'I am the Word. No more sorrows.'

'I am beginning to feel it on my head.'

'Jesus, is this multidimensional?'

'Yes.'

'Is this quantum?'

He replied, 'Yes, but this is the Crown of the Lamb, and it belongs to you, too. I AM the Conquering King.'

'Thank You, Jesus.'

He took both of her hands, and they turned so they were face to face.

She said, 'I have on this crown, He has on His crown, and I'm realizing this is something intimate between the groom and the bride.

'Thank You, Jesus. He's let go of my hands to turn and walk away.'

Jesus said, 'Wear that crown. No more sorrow.'

Stephanie noted, "I'm watching the reverse of the original picture of the storm coming. I'm watching it go backward, and it just stopped raining outside in the natural.

Stephanie asked, "Ron, did we agree with that song, 'Sorrows like see billows roll.' I mean, I know why the guy wrote it. He had just lost his whole family on a ship in a storm, but I'm watching the storm reverse and go backward. I'm watching the water recede and calm down. I'm watching the black clouds and storm clouds leave. Stephanie prayed:

Lord, thank You for being the Conquering King, wearing the Crown of the Lamb, and taking on everything. I often forget that when it talks about 'And by Your stripes we are healed,' it also means emotionally, too. You mean I don't have to take on the sorrow that overwhelms and overcomes us.

You went into the depths of sorrow on my behalf to carry that for us and that we as sons, in alignment and agreement with the Conquering King, inside of the Conquering King, I do not have to be overwhelmed by sorrow and that it can be, as if it never were because of what You did for us that day.

You bore my griefs and carried my sorrows; the chastisement for my peace was upon You so I can have peace. By Your stripes, I am healed, even emotionally. So, I take off sorrow in every age, realm, dimension, and time. I take off the garment of it. I remove the Crown of Sorrows. I won't take it anymore. And for my generations, I ask the angels to go through time.

Father, where we agreed with sorrow or believed it was something we had to endure because of this life, we repent.

Jesus, You said I will have life, and that more abundantly.

I take off that Crown of Sorrows. What You did doesn't include that crown. You said it is not from Your kingdom, sorrow, or being overwhelmed by it. I can grieve without taking on the overwhelming billowing waves and storms of sorrow. So, I repent for where I have fallen short.

I agree with the adversary. I took it on. I allowed it to overwhelm me, and I ask for the blood of Jesus to cover this. I ask for the Amendment of As If It Never Were. I ask for the angels to go through time, on my generational line, and remove the crowns of sorrow, crush them, and bring me the Crown of the Lamb that was slain before the foundations of the world. (Emphasis mine)

Stephanie remarked, "I feel this crown so strongly on my head."

"Remember, you have had sorrow over your previous lifestyle," I commented.

Stephanie said, "For sure."

I continued, "And its impact on your daughters. So, ask Him, how does it impact that?"

Give no place to regret.

Stephanie replied, "I no longer agree with that." I will not agree with sorrow. Regret was one of the things that I believe often accompanies sorrow, and I had already dealt with it. I don't have to be sorry anymore. I don't have to be sorrowful, and I won't. You and Adina don't have to be sorrowful for the things that came against you, the trials you had to endure, and all the betrayal. I don't have to have it, nor do you both have to carry that sorrow. Thank you, Jesus.

I added, "In that passage in Isaiah where it says *bore our griefs*, the word *bore* is also translated, 'To accept, advance, arise, to bring forth, to burn, to carry, to cast, contain, to furnish, to marry."

"Wow!"

Romans 8:18:

> *For I consider that the sufferings of this present time are not worth comparing with* **the glory that is to be revealed to us.** *(Emphasis mine)*

It is being revealed to us! And...

Matthew 5:4:

> *Blessed are those who mourn, for* **they <u>shall</u> be comforted.** *(Emphasis mine)*

"You can't be comforted if you carry sorrow or *have been married* to sorrow. Many people have experienced sorrow and can't seem to find comfort. However, that is the opposite of what the Word says. The Word says (and He *is* the Word) that 'He heals the brokenhearted.'[23] You can't be healed of brokenheartedness or sorrow without realizing He took it to the depths of sorrow. That information CAN end sorrow."

1 Thessalonians 4:13:

But I do not want you to be ignorant, brethren, concerning those who have fallen asleep, lest you sorrow as others who have no hope.

Sorrow can contain hope deferred.

Proverbs 10 22:

*The blessing of the Lord makes rich, and He adds **no sorrow** with it. (Emphasis mine)*

Stephanie continued, "Thank You, Father, for the *Crown of the Lamb*. It is like it was presented today as a gift. He picked it up and put it on His head, but another was on the table. It is the gift of this. We forget that in hell, he went into the depths of sorrow. Thank you, Jesus. Thank you, Jesus."

Generational Crowns of Sorrow

Certain people groups seem to be more prone to sorrow than other people groups. Scotch and Irish

---

[23] Psalm 147:3

people seem to carry sorrow in a way that is uncommon to different groups of people. Throughout the World, certain groups have endured great sorrow that has been passed down from generation to generation. The source of sorrow is not merely environmental, although you can adopt the attitudes of those around you or be influenced by the climate. However, when a spiritual component is in the mix, it creates an inborn dynamic of sorrow and the exhibition of that sorrow in a person's life.

We want to repent for those in our generation who succumbed to the entity of sorrow and come out of partnership with it. It may be due to a hidden nuptial, and a divorce from the entity is in order.

On some, it will manifest as an ownership claim like a Deed of Sorrow or a Lien of Sorrow. In this case, access the Court of Titles and Deeds and either transfer ownership of your life to the Lord Jesus from the entity of sorrow or, if a lien, request that the lien be satisfied by the blood of Jesus.

Another option is simply due to a Crown of Sorrow that one has been living under. In this case, repent for your involvement and remove the Crown of Sorrows from your head. Then, ask for a cleansing of all your realms and healing for the damage to your life that resulted from wearing it. Ask the angels to clear away all the spiritual debris caused by that ungodly crown. Also, request the removal of the Crown of Sorrow from those in your generations.

*Remember, He carried our sorrows,
so we would not have to.*

———— ∞ ————

Chapter 15
Obtaining the
Crown of a Sound Mind

Many people live with a mindset of futility. They have been immersed so thoroughly in a culture that thrives on the Tree of the Knowledge of Good and Evil that they no longer have a sound mind but live with a Crown of Futility of Mind. An exchange must be made.

As I was writing this book, I heard the Father say:

As you dig into more understanding of the crowns and their impact, understand you have just begun to scratch the surface. Many things you thought were just directives are instructions concerning crowns and letting them express dominion in your life.

Father went on to explain some scriptures to me that follow:

For instance, in Ephesians 4:17-24:

17 This I say, therefore, and testify in the Lord, that you should no longer walk as the rest of the Gentiles walk, in the futility of their mind, 18 having their understanding darkened, being alienated from the life of God, because of the ignorance that is in them, because of the blindness of their heart; 19 who, being past feeling, have given themselves over to lewdness, to work all uncleanness with greediness.

He explained,

These have walked under the influence of an inferior crown, a Crown of Futility of Mind, for they have no soundness of mind, are driven by their appetites, have no capacity for reason, and operate in blindness with seared consciences. That inferior crown is reigning in their lives and has yet to be subjected to the Superior Crown found in relationship with Jesus.

Paul continues...

*20 But you have not so learned Christ, 21 if indeed you have heard Him and have been taught by Him, as the truth is in Jesus: (there is a **Crown of Truth** that we should possess) 22 that you put off, (take off every ungodly crown) concerning your former conduct, the old man which grows corrupt according to the deceitful lusts, 23 and be* *renewed in the spirit of your mind, (receive **the Crown of a Sound Mind**) ²⁴ and that you put on the new man which was created according to God, in true righteousness and holiness. (by putting on the **Crown of Righteousness** and living out of Jesus's righteousness) (Emphasis mine)*

Paul explains that when one surrenders to the lordship of Jesus, they will put off the inferior crowns they once wore—the Crown of Wickedness, the Crown of Futility of Mind, and the Crown of Depravity, which brings corruption and animalistic behaviors to fulfill the lusts of the flesh. They put on the Crown of Soundness of Mind, which brings perfect soundness, clarity, peace, and much more. When you put on the 'new man,' you are putting on a new crown that will produce righteousness and true holiness in you.

You have learned about the Crown of Righteousness, but you don't yet know all the workings of it in your life. That is forthcoming and an outworking of that crown in your life. Righteousness is a central attribute of the Kingdom of God. It is how God sees you—righteous.

> *Much of our behavior has been dictated to us by the influence of the wrong crowns. The seven false crowns found in Revelation 12:3:*
>
> *And another sign appeared in heaven: behold, a great, fiery red dragon having seven heads and ten horns, and seven diadems (crowns) on his heads.*

These seven crowns are the culminating crowns by which all other false crowns operate. The seven crowns are:

- The false Crown of Deception (Deceit)
- The false Crown of Fear
- The false Crown of Loathing
- The false Crown of Magic
- The false Crown of Secrets
- The false Crown of Antichrist
- The false Crown of Devouring

They often work together to increase their negative impact on a person. Much of the evil in the world is a result of the activities of the wearers of these crowns. For instance, if the mayor of your town operates under the false Crown of Secrets, he is likely involved in Freemasonry or some similar organization. If he couples that crown with the false Crown of the Antichrist, he is likely to be an antagonist toward committed believers in Jesus, and if he is a churchgoer, he probably is quite religious. He wants things packaged and controlled.

However, if the believers in a city focused intercession efforts to remove the false crowns via intercession and repentance on those in leadership who wear these false crowns, they would instead concentrate on releasing them of the Superior Crowns that Heaven has provided. When you see a church that has minimal or very limited impact, spiritually speaking, you probably could see a churchyard covered in forfeited, lost, or stolen crowns. When you are crownless, you are rudderless.

Many believers have lost the strength that comes with the crowns they once possessed. In my book, *Embracing Your Crown of Authority,* I speak of how to regain lost, forfeited, or stolen crowns. I will insert a summary of those concepts in this book because you need to be able to successfully recover any crowns that you are missing and get the other ones you need.

When we first began teaching about crowns at the end of January 2025, we had no idea that so much information existed about crowns and why they are so vital to the body of Christ. Heaven said this recently:

> *Crowns will cause you to enter new seasons.*

> *Many seasons have been stolen from the sons.*

As you delve into a deeper understanding of the crowns and their impact, realize you have just begun to scratch the surface. Many things you thought were just directives are instructions concerning crowns and letting them express dominion in your life. For instance, in Ephesians 4:17-24:

> *[17] This I say, therefore, and testify in the Lord, that you should no longer walk as the rest of the Gentiles walk, in **the futility of their mind**, [18] **having their understanding darkened**, being alienated from the life of God, because of the ignorance that is in them, **because of the blindness of their heart;** [19] who, being past feeling, have given themselves over to lewdness, to work all uncleanness with greediness. (Emphasis mine)*

These have walked under the influence of an inferior crown, a Crown of Futility of Mind, for they have no soundness of mind, are driven by their appetites, have no capacity for reason, and operate in blindness with seared consciences. That inferior crown is reigning in their lives and has yet to be subjected to the Superior Crown found in relationship with Jesus.

Paul continues...

> *[20] But you have not so learned Christ, [21] if indeed you have heard Him and have been taught by Him, as the truth is in Jesus: (there is a Crown of Truth that we should possess) [22] that you put off,*

(take off every ungodly crown) concerning your former conduct, the old man which grows corrupt according to the deceitful lusts, ²³ *and be renewed in the spirit of your mind, (receive the Crown of a Sound Mind)* ²⁴ *and that you put on the new man which was created according to God, in true righteousness and holiness. (by putting on the Crown of Righteousness and living out of Jesus's righteousness) (Emphasis mine)*

――――― ∞ ―――――

Chapter 16
Maintaining Your Crown

John, the revelator gave us some great insights in how to maintain our crown in Revelation 3:11-12:

¹¹ Do not let tough times make me seem distant from you. I am at hand - see my nearness, not my absence. And don't let temporal setbacks diminish your own authority either. Remember that <u>you call the shots; you wear the crown</u>. My crown endorses your crown. (Lit. Let nothing take your crown.)

¹² It is in your individual, continual association with your victory in me that I will make you to be like a strong pillar in the inner shrine of God's sanctuary, supporting the entire structure of my God-habitation within you. A place to be your permanent abode 'from whence you will never have to depart. And I will engrave upon you the name of my God, also the name of the city [the

bride] of my God, the new Jerusalem that descends from heaven; as well as my own new Name. (MIRROR)

Here are some points to consider:

1. Stay Present to His Nearness

[11] *Do not let tough times make Me seem distant from you. I am at hand—see My nearness, not My absence.*

Insight

- Hard seasons can **cloud your awareness** of God's presence.
- But Jesus reminds us: **He is close**, especially in the struggle.
- Maintaining your crown begins with **maintaining your connection**—staying anchored in intimacy, not circumstances.

How to Apply

- Refuse to interpret delay or pain as abandonment.
- Practice awareness of His nearness in daily life.
- Speak to your soul: *"He is not far. He is here. He is faithful."*

2. Guard Your Authority

¹¹ Don't let temporal setbacks diminish your own authority either. Remember that you call the shots; you wear the crown. (Lit. 'Let no one take your crown.')

Insight

- Crowns represent spiritual authority, identity, and reward.
- Setbacks, criticism, or self-doubt can erode our sense of God-given rule. They are designed to chip away at your assuredness of your authority. Delay is not denial.
- Jesus reminds us that your crown is active <u>now</u>, not just in the age to come.

How to Apply

- Don't hand over your crown through **passivity, fear, or compromise**.
- When attacked, remind yourself: *"I wear a crown. I carry Heaven's backing."*
- **Speak** with authority. **Pray** with confidence. **Walk** like royalty.

---

3. Stand Secure in Union with Christ

¹² It is in your individual, <u>continual association</u> with your victory in Me...

Insight

- Union with Christ is not a one-time moment—it is a **continual, living connection**.
- Victory flows **from Him to you**, not from your effort alone.

How to Apply

- Rehearse your identity daily: "As He is, so am I in this world."[24]
- Refuse **shame, fear**, or **separation-based thinking.**
- **Celebrate your shared victory** with Christ every day. You are co-raised, and co-seated.

---

4. Become a Pillar in His Sanctuary

12 I will make you to be like a strong pillar in the inner shrine...

Insight

- Become unmovable
- You're not just visiting God's presence—you're becoming part of His dwelling. *In you He lives and moves and has His being. (Acts 17:28)*

---

[24] 1 John 4:17

- A pillar supports weight and brings stability—this is a reward of endurance.

How to Apply

- See yourself as a **fixed part of God's house**, not a guest or outsider.
- Endurance today **builds spiritual stature** tomorrow.
- You are **a supporting structure** in the Father's Kingdom on Earth.

---

5. Receive His Names Written on You (Stay firm in your identity which is found in Him).

[12] I will engrave upon you the name of My God... the city of My God... and My own new Name.

Insight

- These engravings speak of **ownership**, **belonging**, and **intimacy**.
- To maintain your crown is to walk **branded by Heaven**, carrying its identity and authority.

How to Apply

- Declare: "I am marked by God. I belong to Heaven. His Name is on me."

- Let your life reveal His nature—His character etched in your actions.
- You are not nameless—you are named **by the King.**

Summary: How to Maintain Your Crown

Principle	Action
Stay near	Don't let trials blind you to His presence
Guard your crown	Walk in your God-given authority, don't forfeit it
Abide in victory	Stay joined to Christ's triumph daily
Be unshakable	Let endurance make you a pillar in God's house
Live marked	Carry His Name, His city, and His Glory on your life

Activation Prayer

Father, thank You for placing a crown upon my head—a crown of righteousness, life, and glory.

Teach me to walk worthy of it.

I repent for any time I have dishonored or neglected what You entrusted to me.

By Your grace, I choose to hold fast, walk in humility, and live faithfully before You.

Help me to endure, to resist temptation, and to honor You in everything.

May no one take my crown.

In Jesus' name, Amen.

———— ∞ ————

Chapter 17

Epilogue

Many believers have lost the strength that comes with the crowns they once possessed. In my book, *Embracing Your Crown of Authority*, I discuss how to regain lost, forfeited, or stolen crowns. This book was about understanding the various components within each crown that are yours to maximize. I included a summary of these concepts in this book, as you must be able to successfully recover any missing crowns and obtain the others you require.

Understanding what has been lost is crucial to regaining the footing you may have had in times past, knowing that the Father has the capability to make the negatives in your past as if they never happened. Combining the understanding of crowns with the operation of the Courts of Heaven will help solidify both the recovery of lost crowns and the commissioning of new ones. This book was designed to guide you in making significant progress on that journey.

Court Scenario on Your Behalf

Father, I request entrance to the Court of Crowns for the sons reading this book today. I ask that their Registry of Crowns be readily available and open to them so they may see what crowns they have been destined to receive, what crowns have been lost, forfeited, or stolen, and what the status of some of the neglected crowns is so they can proactively utilize them for the sake of the Kingdom of Heaven.

May they regain every lost or forfeited crown. May they gain every crown they need at this time in their life, and may they step into the authorization of the Father for every crown.

May every false crown be removed from their lives, along with every false mantle, throne, anointing, dominion, scepter, and all false resources, and may they be destroyed by fire.

May the angels of Heaven be released to clear up all spiritual debris from these false crowns, and may they step into the fullness of the authority of every crown they possess as sons and gain every crown they are to have. Thank you, Father.

———— ∞ ————

Appendix

Learning to Live Spirit First

A challenge with how we were taught about the Christian life is that everything was put off until sometime in the future. Then, we read Paul's letters and experienced a disconnect. Heaven, to us, was a destination, not a resource. We knew nothing about learning to live from our spirits. We only knew what we had been doing since birth, and that was to live to satisfy our soul or flesh. We sorely need to learn an alternative way of living.

Exchanging Our Way of Living

Paul recorded these words in his letter to the Romans:

Romans 8:5:

> *Those who are motivated by the flesh only pursue what benefits themselves. But those who live by the impulses of the Holy Spirit are motivated to pursue spiritual realities.*

We must learn to live spirit first! We must exchange our way of living. We must learn to live from our spirit. We need to understand the hierarchy within us:

    a. We are a spirit.
    b. We possess a soul.
    c. We live in a body.

Each component has a specific purpose in our lives. Our spirit is the interface with the supernatural realm. It is designed for interfacing with Heaven and the Kingdom realm. Our spirit has been in existence in our body since conception. Our soul has a different purpose. It communicates to our intellect and our physical body what our spirit has obtained from Heaven. It is the interface with our body. Our body houses the two components and follows the dictates of whichever component is dominating,

Most of us have never been taught about having our spirit dominate. Rather, we have merely assumed that our soul being dominant was the required mode of operation.

Our soul always wants to be in charge. Our soul is susceptible to carnal or fleshly desires, lusts, and behaviors. It will, at times, resist our spirit and body. It must be made to submit to our spirit by an act of our will.

Our will is a means of instructing either component (spirit, soul, or body) in what to do. Our soul has a will, and so does our spirit. We choose who dominates!

Our body, on the other hand, has appetites that will control us in subjection to our soul. They become partners in crime—remember that second piece of chocolate cake it wanted? Our body will try, along with our soul, to dictate our behavior. It will likely resist the spirit's domination of our lives. However, it will obey our spirit's domination if instructed, and our body can aid our spirit if trained to do so.

The typical expression that operates in most people's lives is that their soul is first, body second, and their spirit is somewhere in the distance in last place.

In some people, especially those very conscious of their physical fitness or physical appearance, there is a different lineup. Their body is their priority, the soul second, and again, their spirit is the lowest priority.

Heaven's desire for us is vastly different. Heaven desires that we live spirit first, soul second, and body third. Since we are spiritual beings, this is the optimal arrangement. For most of us, our spirit was not activated in our lives in any measure until we became born again.

If, after our salvation experience, we began to pursue our relationship with the Father, then we became much more aware of our spirit and learned to live more spirit-conscious. The apostle Paul wrote in his various epistles about living in the spirit or walking in the spirit.

Because we are spiritual beings, our spirits cry out for a deepening of relationship with the Father.

Our spirit longs for it and will try to steer us in that direction. Many of us had a hunger for God from early in our lives.

Our soul has certain characteristics that explain its behavior in our life. This is the briefest of lists, but I think we will get the idea. Our soul is selfish. It wants what it wants when it wants it. It can be very pouty. It can act like a small child. It is offendable and often even looks for opportunities to be offended. Our soul is also rude.

Our body has a different set of characteristics. It is inconsiderate, demanding, lazy, and self-serving. It does not want to get out of bed in the morning, for many people. In others, it wants to be fed things that are not beneficial.

However, the characteristics of our spirit are hugely different. If we live out of our spirit, we will find that we are loving and prone to be gentle. We desire peace. We are considerate. We are far more contented when living out of our spirit. Also, joy will often have a great expression in our lives.

Sometimes, we have experienced traumas that create a situation of our soul not trusting our spirit. The soul blames the spirit for not protecting it. The irony is that, typically, our soul never gave place to the spirit so that it could protect us. The soul places false blame on the spirit, and it must be coerced to forgive the spirit. Then, the soul must relinquish control to the spirit. Once the soul forgives the spirit, the two components can begin to work in harmony.

If I were to flash an image of some delicious, freshly cooked donuts in front of us, what would happen? For many, their body would announce a craving for one. What if, instead, I showed an image of a bowl of broccoli? How many people would get excited about that? Probably not as much excitement over a bowl of broccoli would be exhibited. Which does our body prefer—the donuts or broccoli? For the untamed soul, the donuts are likely to win out every time. Which do most kids prefer?

In any case, we can train ourselves to go for the healthier option. A principle regarding this that I heard years ago is summed up like this:

What we feed will live—
what we starve will die

What do we want to be dominant—our spirit, our soul, or our body? The part we feed is the part that will dominate.

For some, they feed their soul and live by the logic of their mind. Everything must be reasoned out in their mind before they will accept it. However, because our soul gains its insight from the Tree of the Knowledge of Good and Evil, it will always have faulty and limited understandings.

How do we change this soul-dominant or body-dominant pattern? We instruct our soul to back up, and we call our spirit to come forward. Some people may need to physically stand up and speak to our soul and say, "Soul, back up," and as they say those words, take a physical step backward. Then, speak to their spirit out loud and say, "Spirit, come forward." As we speak those words, take a physical step forward. This prophetic act helps trigger a shift within them.

Live spirit first!

Benefits of Living Spirit First

Why would we want to live spirit first? Let me present several reasons. Living spirit first will create in us an increased awareness of Heaven and the realms of Heaven. It will create a deeper comprehension of the presence of Holy Spirit, of angels, and men and women in white linen. We will be able to better hear the voice of Heaven. We will experience greater creativity, productivity, hope, and peace. We will become more aware of the needs of people that we meet.

> *As we live spirit first, we will be able to access the riches of Heaven in our life.*

Petty things that formerly bothered us will dissipate in importance or impact in our lives. We will be able to move ahead, not concerned with the petty, mundane, or unproductive things that have affected our lives before we begin to live spirit first.

This way of life is more than a game changer—for the believer, it is the only way to live. We will face challenges as we build our business or live our life from Heaven down, but we will more readily be able to access the solutions of Heaven as we live with an awareness of the richness of Heaven and all that is available to us as a son or daughter of the Lord Most High. Do not live dominated by the soul.

> Live **spirit** first!

———— ∞ ————

Resources from
LifeSpring International Ministries

A visit to the **RonHorner.com** website will give a glimpse of the various branches of ministry we are involved in. We started by providing coaching to people within the Courts of Heaven, advocating for them and their situations. Our corporate name is LifeSpring International Ministries, Inc., a North Carolina registered nonprofit.

Personal Advocacy Sessions

Known as Personal Advocacy Sessions, these 90-minute sessions with our trained team of advocates have successfully worked with a myriad of situations. If you have an issue that you can't seem to get breakthrough about, schedule a session with our advocates.

LifeSpring Mentoring Group

Since starting this weekly class on Zoom in 2019, we have taught on the Courts of Heaven, protocols, engaging Heaven for revelation, working with angels and men and women in white linen, lingering human spirits, and more. It is a free class. Simply visit **ronhorner.com** to register for the link for the class.

Membership Program

We have several tiers of membership for those tracking with us. The Platinum level gains you access to our library of videos, blogs, and more. Again, visit the website.

LifeSpring School of Ministry

A trimester-based school to help you grow in your walk. Trimester 1 focuses on cleansing your generations. Trimester 2 focuses on Protocols of the Courts of Heaven, and Trimester 3 focuses on Advanced Protocols of the Courts of Heaven. Completion of Trimesters 1, 2, and 3 will qualify the student for consideration as a Junior or Senior Advocate able to conduct Personal Advocacy Sessions with our clients.

CourtsNet

CourtsNet is our video-based training program offering a wide variety of classes and courses. We have free courses as well as paid courses.

AfterCare

Not every situation is solved by the Courts of Heaven. Sometimes people need to learn simple things to navigate life. Our AfterCare program provides Biblical counseling, classes, and groups regularly.

Sandhills Ecclesia

In 2022, we began a Sunday Gathering known as Sandhills Ecclesia, which is the name we saw on the book in Heaven when we went to inquire. My wife, Adina, and I live in the North Carolina area known as the Sandhills region, hence the name. We meet weekly at 11:00 AM Eastern Time, and on the first Sunday of each month, we have an afternoon gathering to conduct legislative work in the Courts of Heaven as a group. All are welcome. Simply visit **sandhillsecclesia.com** and register for the link.

Heaven Down Business

Heaven Down Business is a worldwide coaching and consultancy business designed to assist entrepreneurs and business owners in implementing the Heaven Down™ Business Building paradigm into their business. For more information, visit **heavendownbusiness.com**.

Adina's Melodies/Heaven Down Music

Adina Horner, co-founder, is a gifted minstrel and has several albums of prophetic worship music available on several of the most popular music platforms. Visit **adinasmelodies.com**.

LifeSpring Publishing/Scroll Publishers

LifeSpring Publishing primarily publishes Dr. Ron's books, and Scroll Publishers is our imprint where we publish the books of others relating to engaging Heaven, living spirit forward, and the Heaven Down™ lifestyle.

YouTube Channel

Our most recent videos from the Mentoring Group are posted on YouTube®. Visit our YouTube® channel,

courtsofheavenwebinar on YouTube® for the latest videos.

RonHorner.com

Our website, **RonHorner.com,** has a myriad of resources, many of which are free, as well as numerous videos.

———— ∞ ————

Description

In *Maximizing Your Crown of Authority*, step into a powerful heavenly encounter where the prophet Ezekiel pierces a radiant star, releasing a golden, living liquid that pours into crowns upon the heads of God's sons and daughters across the Earth.

As angels descend for battle and the heavens resound with glory, a deeper mystery is revealed: each crown is a vessel—unique, sacred, and filled with a personalized outpouring from the Trinity.

Guided by Lady Wisdom and Holy Spirit, this revelatory journey unveils the cosmic battle over your God-given authority. You will discover how your crown carries divine purpose, how your words empower angelic hosts, and how what fills your crown determines whether you rule with light or fall into darkness.

This is not just a vision—it is a summons: a call to awaken to the truth of who you are, what you've been given, and how Heaven partners with you to bring transformation to the Earth. Satan fears the authority you carry. Heaven is waiting for you to walk in it.

You were born crowned. Now, it's time to understand what has been poured into yours—and why it changes everything.

———— ∞ ————

About the Author

Dr. Ron Horner is an apostolic teacher specializing in the Courts of Heaven. He has written nearly forty books on the Courts of Heaven, engaging Heaven, working with angels, living from revelation, and most recently on Crowns of Authority.

He currently trains people in engaging the Courts of Heaven in a weekly online teaching session. You can register to participate and discover more about the Courts of Heaven prayer paradigm on his various websites, classes, products, and services found here:

www.ronhorner.com

──── ∞ ────

Other Books by Dr. Ron M. Horner

Building Your Business from Heaven Down

Building Your Business from Heaven Down 2.0

Building Your Business with the Blueprint of Heaven

Commissioning Angels – Volume 1

Cooperating with the Glory

Courts of Heaven Process Charts

Dealing with Trusts & Consequential Liens

Embracing Your Crown of Authority

Embracing Crowns for Governmental Intercession

Embracing Crowns for Your Business

Embracing Crowns for Your Family

Engaging Angels in the Realms of Heaven

Engaging Heaven for Revelation – Volume 1

Engaging Heaven for Revelation – Volume 2

Engaging Heaven for Trade

Engaging the Courts for Ownership & Order

Engaging the Courts for Your City (*Paperback, Leader's Guide & Workbook*)

Engaging the Courts of Healing & the Healing Garden

Engaging the Courts of Heaven

Engaging the Help Desk of the Courts of Heaven

Four Keys to Dismantling Accusations

Freedom from Mithraism

Kingdom Dynamics – Volume 1

Kingdom Dynamics – Volume 2

Let's Get it Right!

Lingering Human Spirits

Lingering Human Spirits – Volume 2

Living Spirit Forward

Maximizing Your Crown of Authority

Next Dimension Access to the Court of Supplications

Overcoming the False Verdicts of Freemasonry

Overcoming Verdicts from the Courts of Hell

Releasing Bonds from the Courts of Heaven

The Courts of Heaven: An Introduction
(formerly *Engaging the Mercy Court of Heaven*)

Unlocking Spiritual Seeing

Working with Your Realms and Your Realm Angels

SPANISH

Cómo Anular los Falsos Veredictos de la Masonería

Cómo Proceder en la Corte Celestial de Misericordia

Cómo Proceder en las Cortes para su Ciudad

Cómo Trabajar con Angeles en los Ambitos del Cielo

Cooperando con La Gloria de Dios

Las Cuatro Llaves para Anular las Acusaciones

Liberando Bonos en las Cortes Celestiales

Liberando Su Visión Espiritual

Sea Libre del Mitraísmo

Tablas de Proceso de la Cortes del Cielo

———— ∞ ————

Notes

Notes

www.ingramcontent.com/pod-product-compliance
Lightning Source LLC
Chambersburg PA
CBHW022006160426
43197CB00007B/292